Social Security Disability Insurance

Social Security Disability Insurance

The Problems of Unexpected Growth

Charles W. Meyer

American Enterprise Institute for Public Policy Research
Washington, D.C.

Charles W. Meyer is professor of economics at Iowa State University.

ISBN 0–8847–3365–2

Library of Congress Catalog Card No. 79–24153

AEI Studies 262

Printed in the United States of America

CONTENTS

6 PROPOSALS FOR REVISING THE DISABILITY INSURANCE SYSTEM   54

Program Changes 54
Administrative Changes 60
Other Reforms 64

LIST OF TABLES

1
Introduction

Disability insurance (DI), which was added to the Social Security System in 1956, provides monthly cash benefits for insured persons who are totally disabled. In addition, persons receiving DI benefits for a period of two consecutive years or more are granted hospital and supplementary insurance protection under medicare. The amount of the monthly disability insurance benefits received by persons varies. Like old age and survivors benefits, the amount received is based on a worker's average monthly earnings in covered employment.

There are three categories of disabled recipients:

- Insured workers under age sixty-five who become totally disabled for a period of one year or more. The spouse of a worker receiving DI benefits is also eligible for a spouse's benefit if the spouse cares for a child under age eighteen, is disabled, or is over age sixty-two. In addition, unmarried children of a disabled worker are eligible for dependent's benefits up to age eighteen, and up to age twenty-two if in school.

- Disabled widows, widowers, or divorced wives aged fifty to fifty-nine who meet other requirements for widow's or widower's benefits. Because these benefits are paid at an earlier age than survivor's benefits, they are actuarially reduced.

- Disabled sons or daughters of a worker entitled to disability or retirement benefits. To qualify, the son or daughter must have become disabled before reaching age twenty-two. These childhood disability benefits are payable as early as age eighteen.

Payments to the disabled and their dependents have quadrupled from about $3 billion in 1970 to nearly $12 billion in 1978. During that same period, the total number of beneficiaries has increased from 2.7 million to 4.9 million, of whom 2.9 million are disabled workers, 1.5 million are

1

dependent children, and 0.5 million are spouses of disabled workers. In August 1978, the average monthly payment to workers in current payment status was $286.34; the average award to new workers entering the program was $326.82, reflecting the higher average earnings of recent entrants.

Most disability benefits are paid out of a DI trust fund that is separate from the Old Age and Survivors Insurance (OASI) trust fund. Approximately 12 percent of social security payroll tax revenue is allocated to the disability fund; the remainder (excluding medicare) goes into the OASI fund. Benefits for disabled widows and widowers (survivors of beneficiaries) and qualifying disabled children aged eighteen and over are paid out of the OASI fund.

The rapid growth in the number of DI beneficiaries that occurred during the early and mid-1970s pushed costs well above projected levels and forced Congress in 1977 to increase the flow of payroll tax revenues into the DI trust fund. The growth rate in the number of beneficiaries has slowed recently, but the high cost and anticipated future growth in the program is still a matter of concern.

Many disabled workers are so severely impaired that they could not work under any circumstances. Those with residual marketable skills could perhaps become self-supporting if they are given the proper economic incentives, job opportunities, and rehabilitation services. Critics of the DI program have proposed a variety of program changes designed to reduce work disincentives without adding unduly to the financial strains on beneficiaries.

Another source of concern is the way claims for disability benefits are processed. Unlike social security retirement benefits, which depend on age and earnings history, disability awards are based on judgments about an individual's physical or mental condition. The development of a set of criteria that can be used to decide who qualifies for benefits and who does not is a most challenging exercise in public administration. The goal is to establish a set of determination procedures that can be applied equitably and expeditiously to the approximately 1.2 million claims that are filed each year.

2

The Evolution of Disability Insurance

Disability insurance coverage has been broadened and eligibility requirements have been relaxed since the program was established in 1956. Benefit levels have risen rapidly, especially in the last decade.

Legislative History

During the formative years of social security in the 1930s, no serious attempt was made to include disability insurance in the program. The need for income replacement for workers who become disabled was recognized, but this consideration was overridden by uncertainty about the cost of a disability program. In contrast to OASI, eligibility for DI benefits is complicated to measure and the number qualifying is difficult to predict. The disastrous experience with private disability insurance during the Depression added to these fears.

Support for inclusion of disability insurance broadened during the 1940s. Annual reports of the Social Security Board (predecessor of the Social Security Administration) recommended benefits for permanently and totally disabled persons who had significant experience in the labor force. The 1948 report of the Advisory Council on Social Security to the Senate Finance Committee contained many recommendations later incorporated in the DI program. In 1949, the House of Representatives passed an amendment to the Social Security Act that included a DI program, but the Senate rejected this House version.

A major legislative breakthrough occurred in 1954 when Congress introduced the disability "freeze." Under the freeze, the quarters during which a worker is disabled are not counted in determining the number of quarters needed to be fully or currently insured under OASI, and the years in which a worker is disabled are excluded from OASI benefit

3

calculations. The freeze is intended to protect workers from loss or reduction of retirement and survivor benefits because of inability to work during periods of disability. This legislation is important because it established criteria for determining disability status and required that administrative machinery be created to process claims. Eligibility for freeze status was limited to workers with a minimum of twenty quarters of covered employment in the forty-quarter period ending with the onset of disability, including six of the thirteen quarters ending with the onset. The disability was to be of prolonged and indeterminate duration, medically demonstrable, and of sufficient severity to prevent the worker from performing any gainful activity.

Congress specified that the initial determination of disability be made by state vocational rehabilitation agencies operating in accordance with federal standards. It was hoped that bringing the disabled into contact with state rehabilitation agencies would encourage them to take advantage of agency services. In addition, the well-established relationships between state agencies and the medical profession would aid in the determination process. The introduction of the freeze brought into being the joint state-federal apparatus for determining disability that exists today.

Once the administrative apparatus was in operation, a major obstacle to disability insurance was removed, and the DI program was added to social security in 1956. To qualify for benefits a claimant must be found unable to engage in any substantial gainful activity by reason of any medically determinable physical or mental impairment expected to result in death or to be of long or indefinite duration. Benefits were restricted to workers aged fifty to sixty-five and to disabled dependent children of retired or deceased insured workers if disabled before age eighteen.[1] To attain insured status under DI, one must have worked in covered employment during twenty of the last forty and six of the last thirteen quarters ending with the quarter of onset of disability. Benefits could begin only after a wait of at least six months after onset. As in the case of retirement, benefit levels were a function of average monthly earnings in covered employment and could be reduced on a dollar-for-dollar basis if the individual was receiving disability benefits from another federal program or payments under workmen's compensation. Beneficiaries were to be screened for rehabilitation potential, and benefits could be terminated for refusal to accept rehabilitation services from state agencies.

The basic features of the original program remain, but the initial

---

[1] Benefits to dependent children are now limited to those who became disabled before age twenty-two.

legislation has been subject to several important amendments. These include elimination of the benefit reduction for those receiving other federal disability or workmen's compensation benefits (1958), elimination of the recency-of-work provision that required covered employment in six of thirteen quarters at time of onset (1958), and elimination of the minimum age requirement of fifty (1960). The 1960 amendments included two provisions designed to encourage beneficiaries to try returning to work. A trial work period of nine months, not necessarily consecutive, allows workers who still meet the criteria for benefits to attempt to work without loss of benefits. If at the conclusion of the trial period the worker is found to be able to engage in substantial gainful activity, his benefits will be terminated after an additional three months. A second provision allows disabled workers who return to beneficiary status to receive benefits immediately rather than after a six-month waiting period.

The 1965 amendments liberalized eligibility standards by replacing the requirement that the disability be of "long-continued and indefinite duration" with the requirement that it be expected to last for a continuous period of twelve months or longer. Eligibility requirements for blind workers were also relaxed. A benefit offset for state workmen's compensation benefits, which had been removed in 1958, was reinserted. The new provision limited the combined total of monthly workmen's compensation plus DI benefit payments to 80 percent of average current earnings before disability. To encourage increased efforts at rehabilitation, the 1965 amendments authorized the use of money from the DI trust fund to reimburse state vocational rehabilitation agencies for the cost of services furnished to beneficiaries.

In 1967, after a series of liberalizing amendments, Congress acted for the first time to tighten eligibility requirements. The number of disability allowances exceeded estimates, and this was attributed to liberal rulings by the courts. It was feared that these rulings could lead to substantial cost overruns, particularly if they were incorporated in administrative guidelines. The most significant of numerous court cases, *Kerner v. Flemming*, established the influential "Kerner doctrine," which held that the theoretical ability to work was not sufficient cause to deny benefits.[2] *Kerner* and subsequent cases placed on the government the burden of proof to show that work that the claimant could perform was available in the area where he lived. At the same time, courts were relaxing the criteria for establishing mental and physical disability as prescribed in Social Security Administration regulations. As a result, DI was becoming a form of unemployment insurance for persons whose ability to work was affected by mental or physical impairments.

---

[2] Kerner v. Flemming, 283 F. 2d 916 (2d. Cir. 1960).

The 1967 amendments reworded the statutory definition of disability to require physical or mental impairments that—considering age, education, and work experience—prevent a claimant from engaging "in any kind of substantial gainful work which exists in the national economy, regardless of whether such work exists in the area in which he lives, or whether a specific job vacancy exists for him, or whether he would be hired if he applied for work."[3] The report of the conference committee that reconciled the House and Senate versions of the amendments interprets the references to "national economy" as meaning "work which exists in significant numbers either in the region where the individual lives or in several regions of the country."[4] The 1967 amendments also emphasized the importance of medical factors in disability by limiting physical and mental impairments to those that "are demonstrable by medically acceptable clinical and laboratory diagnostic techniques."

Although the 1967 amendments tightened the definition of disability, they continued the liberalization of coverage. Workers under age thirty-one became eligible if they worked in covered employment for one-half of the quarters between age twenty-one and onset of disability, with a minimum of six quarters. Coverage was extended to disabled widows and dependent disabled widowers of insured workers. In addition, the 1967 amendments authorized the Secretary of Health, Education, and Welfare to reimburse attorneys' fees of claimants in administrative proceedings that result in a ruling in favor of the claimant.

The trend toward liberalization continued with passage of the 1972 amendments. Among the changes were a reduction in the waiting period for benefits from six months after onset to five and a relaxation in the recency-of-work and quarters-of-coverage requirements for blind persons. In addition, recipients were made eligible for medicare coverage to begin after twenty-four consecutive months on the benefit roll.

The 1977 Amendments

By 1977, the entire social security system faced a funding crisis, and Congress was forced to act. Actuarial estimates indicated that the OASI trust fund would be exhausted in the early 1980s. The DI trust fund was in even worse shape, with depletion expected by the end of 1978. Congress responded by passing the Social Security Amendments of 1977. A sizable increase in social security taxes relieved the short-term

---

[3] U.S. Congress, House of Representatives, Committee on Ways and Means, *Committee Staff Report on the Disability Insurance Program*, 93d Congress, 2d session, July 1974, p. 117.
[4] Ibid.

TABLE 1

DISABILITY INSURANCE TAX RATES ON BOTH EMPLOYEES AND EMPLOYERS
UNDER 1977 AMENDMENTS AND PRIOR LAW
(percent)

| | 1977 Amendments | | Prior Law | | |
| | Tax rate on both employee and employer | Percentage of social security tax revenue to DI | Tax rate on both employee and employer | Percentage of social security tax revenue to DI | Tax Rate Increase as a Percentage of Prior Rate |
Year					
1977	0.575	9.8	0.575	9.8	—
1978	0.775	12.8	0.6	9.9	29.2
1979–1980	0.75	12.2	0.6	9.9	25.0
1981	0.825	12.4	0.65	10.3	26.9
1982–1984	0.825	12.3	0.65	10.3	26.9
1985	0.95	13.5	0.65	10.3	46.2
1986–1989	0.95	13.3	0.7	10.9	35.7
1990–2010	1.1	14.4	0.7	10.9	57.1
2011 and later	1.1	14.4	0.85	11.4	29.4

SOURCE: Social Security Amendments of 1977, Public Law 95–216, 91 Stat. 1510–1512.

funding crisis, while a change in the method of calculating benefits reduced but did not eliminate the anticipated long-term deficit.

Current Funding for DI. The 1977 amendments raised the payroll tax rates for DI 25 to 30 percent above the previously legislated levels for the years 1978 through 1984. Much larger increases are contemplated for the 1985–2010 period. Because the rate increase for the DI component is greater than the increases for OASI and health insurance, the share of tax revenue allocated to disability is increased. In recognition of the precarious state of the DI trust fund, Congress increased the share of tax revenue going to disability from 9.8 percent of taxes on employers and employees in 1977 to 12.8 percent in 1978. As shown in Table 1, this share dropped to 12.2 percent in 1979 but will rise gradually to 14.4 percent in 1990.

Table 2 shows a similar pattern of rate and share increases for the self-employed. Rate increases are greater for the self-employed than for other workers after 1980. The rate on the self-employed was set at 75 percent of the combined rate on employees and employers, reestablishing the ratio that existed until 1972.

TABLE 2

DISABILITY INSURANCE TAX RATES ON THE SELF-EMPLOYED UNDER 1977
AMENDMENTS AND PRIOR LAW
(percent)

| | 1977 Amendments | | Prior Law | | |
| | Tax rate on self-employed | Percentage of social security tax revenue to DI | Tax rate on self-employed | Percentage of social security tax revenue to DI | Tax Rate Increase as a Percentage of Prior Rate |
Year					
1977	0.815	10.3	0.815	10.3	—
1978	1.09	13.5	0.85	10.5	28.2
1979–1980	1.04	12.8	0.85	10.5	22.4
1981	1.2375	13.3	0.92	11.0	34.5
1982–1984	1.2375	13.2	0.92	11.0	34.5
1985	1.425	14.4	0.92	11.0	50.5
1986–1989	1.425	14.2	0.99	11.6	43.9
1990–2010	1.65	15.3	0.99	11.6	66.7
2011 and later	1.65	15.3	1.0	11.8	65.0

SOURCE: Social Security Amendments of 1977, Public Law 95–216, 91 Stat. 1510–1512.

TABLE 3

COMBINED EMPLOYEE-EMPLOYER DISABILITY INSURANCE TAX UNDER 1977
AMENDMENTS IN 1977, 1981, AND 1988
(dollars)

| | Year | | | Percentage Increase from 1977 to 1988 |
Earnings	1977	1981	1988	
$10,000	115.00	165.00	190.00	65
16,500 [a]	189.75	272.25	313.50	65
20,000	189.75	330.00	380.00	100
29,700 [b]	189.75	490.05	564.30	197
47,100 [c]	189.75	490.05	894.90	372

[a] Maximum taxable earnings in 1977.
[b] Maximum taxable earnings in 1981.
[c] Estimated maximum taxable earnings in 1988.
SOURCE: Calculated from U.S. Congress, House of Representatives, Committee on Ways and Means, Social Security Financing, 95th Congress, 2d session, May 10, 1978, p. 4.

The rate increases are augmented by substantial increases in the annual earnings base subject to the social security tax. Current law raises the taxable limit from $17,700 in 1978 to $29,700 in 1981 via annual increments of from $3,000 to $5,200. After 1981, the taxable earnings base will increase automatically in line with changes in average earnings in covered employment. One consequence of the hike in the taxable limit is a rather disparate pattern of tax increases for different earnings levels, with greater increases for persons with higher incomes. Table 3 gives examples of the impact of the DI tax component on persons with annual earnings of $10,000, $20,000, and at or above the taxable limit for the years 1977, 1981, and 1988. Amounts are for the combined tax on employers and employees. Because of the combined effect of higher rates and earnings limits, the maximum possible increase in the DI tax component between 1977 and 1988 is 372 percent. This increase applies to earnings at or above the projected 1988 taxable maximum, which is estimated to be at $47,100. In contrast, the tax on earnings at or below the 1977 maximum taxable earnings of $16,500 increase only 65 percent over the same period.

TABLE 4

PRELIMINARY ESTIMATES OF THE OPERATIONS OF THE DISABILITY
INSURANCE TRUST FUND UNDER PRESENT LAW, 1977–1988
(billions of dollars)

Year	Income	Outgo	Net Change	Fund at End of Year
1977	9.6	11.9	− 2.4	3.4
1978	13.8	13.3	0.5	3.8
1979	15.7	15.2	0.5	4.3
1980	17.6	17.1	0.5	4.8
1981	21.4	19.0	2.4	7.2
1982	23.8	21.0	2.8	10.0
1983	26.1	23.2	3.0	13.0
1984	28.2	25.4	2.8	15.7
1985	34.4	27.6	6.8	22.6
1986	37.6	30.0	7.6	30.2
1987	40.5	32.5	8.0	38.2
1988	43.6	35.3	8.3	46.5

SOURCE: U.S. Congress, House of Representatives, Committee on Ways and Means, *Social Security Financing,* 95th Congress, 2d session, May 10, 1978, p. 8.

Under current law, the maximum projected tax payable into the disability fund alone in 1988 will be $894.90. In contrast, as recently as 1972 the maximum tax for all three components of the social security program—old age and survivors, disability, and health—was $828.

Outlook for the DI Trust Fund. The immediate effect of the new funding arrangements is to avert the impending crisis in the DI trust fund. As shown in Table 4, the $2.4 billion deficit of 1977 is followed by estimated surpluses of $500 million for the next three years and much larger surpluses thereafter. These projections are from the Office of the Actuary of the Social Security Administration and are based on an "intermediate" set of economic assumptions for the years 1978–1988.[5]

The long-term prospects for the fund are more clouded. An actuarial projection by the Social Security Administration shows the fund in surplus for about two decades and in deficit thereafter despite an increase in the DI tax rate from the combined rate of 1.5 percent of taxable earnings on employees and employers in 1979 to a rate of 2.2 percent beginning in 1990.[6] These projections are highly sensitive to assumptions about trends in prices, wages, employment, and demographic variables, but they indicate that future adjustments in taxes or benefit levels may be necessary.

---

[5] U.S. Congress, House of Representatives, Committee on Ways and Means, *Social Security Financing*, 95th Congress, 2d session, May 10, 1978, p. 2.

[6] Ibid., pp. 4, 12.

3

Qualifying for Benefits

To be eligible for disability benefits under social security, a worker must meet three conditions. He must have insured status; present evidence of total, long-term disability; and complete a five-month waiting period following the onset of disability. The administrative tasks of determining who is insured and confirming compliance with the waiting period are relatively simple, but the task of determining whether an applicant meets the statutory requirements of total disability is much more complex. The statutory definition of disability is sufficiently imprecise to require a time-consuming evaluation of the evidence in the many borderline cases.

The Social Security Administration (SSA) has created an elaborate federal-state administrative apparatus to handle the more than 1.2 million claims that are filed each year and to reevaluate previous awards to claimants who show some rehabilitation potential.

Processing Claims for Disabled Worker's Benefits

The process of applying for benefits begins with the filing of a claim at an SSA district office. The applicant provides information on age, work history, and sources of medical data.

Insured Status. To be eligible for benefits, a worker must be "fully insured" under OASDHI. Fully insured status is attained by working in covered employment at least one quarter for each year since 1950 or since age twenty-one (if later). A worker with forty quarters of coverage is fully insured for life. In addition, a worker must have disability-insured status. For a worker aged thirty-one or over, this requires covered employment in twenty of the last forty quarters ending with the quarter of onset of the disability. This test is designed to establish how recently the worker was attached to the labor force. Workers aged thirty or under are granted insured status for DI if they worked in covered employment in at least half of the quarters since they reached age twenty-one, with a minimum of six quarters of coverage. The requirement of recent labor force attachment is waived for the blind, who are granted insured status on the basis of from six to forty quarters of covered employment, depending on the age when blindness occurred. About 20 percent of claims are denied owing to lack of insured status.

Determination of Disability. As soon as SSA determines that a claimant has insured status, it notifies the state vocational rehabilitation agency in the claimant's state of residence. In an effort to tie the DI program into state efforts at vocational rehabilitation, Congress specified that the initial determination of disability be made at the state level. The state agency obtains medical data from sources provided by the SSA and may require the applicant to submit to an additional medical examination. State agencies must make their determinations in accordance with federal statutes and SSA regulations. For purposes of entitlement to disabled worker's benefits, disability is defined as:

> The inability to engage in any substantial gainful activity by reason of any medically determinable physical or mental impairment which can be expected to result in death or which has lasted or can be expected to last for a continuous period of not less than 12 months. A person must be not only unable to do his previous work in amount of earnings and utilization but cannot, considering his age, education, and work experience, engage in any other kind of substantial gainful work which exists in the national economy, regardless of whether such work exists in the immediate area in which he lives, or whether a specific job vacancy exists for him, or whether he would be hired if he applied for work. [1]

In general terms, this means that an insured person must have a physical or mental impairment severe enough to rule out significant gainful employment. In effect, the recipient of DI benefits must be found to be totally disabled for a period of at least one year.

The criteria cited in the definition given above have been clarified to varying degrees by administrative regulations and practice and by court decisions. Nevertheless, judgments in individual cases are often quite subjective.

---

[1] Social Security Act, Sections 216(i)(1), 223(d)(2)(A); *Code of Federal Regulations*, Title 20, Part 404.1502, pp. 340–41.

Actual earnings are regarded as evidence of ability to engage in "substantial gainful activity," and under current regulations benefits are denied or terminated (after a trial work period) if earnings exceed $280 a month, regardless of an individual's medical status. In some cases, earnings of less than $280 a month may be interpreted as implying substantial gainful activity and may thus serve as a basis for denying benefits.

In the absence of significant earnings, state agencies must rely on other data relating to a claimant's medical condition and residual employability. Robert G. Dixon, Jr., has identified three tests, successively more subjective, that may be inferred from federal regulations.[2]

The first test is a list of major physical and mental impairments that will automatically qualify a claimant for benefits. Examples include progressive and uncontrolled cancer, serious cardiovascular disease, and loss of both arms, both legs, or an arm and a leg. A claimant whose impairment is not on the list may qualify if the impairment is judged to be medically equivalent to one that is listed. An element of subjectivity is therefore present even under this most objective of tests.

A second test involves what Dixon aptly describes as the "worn-out" manual labor syndrome.[3] A person with long-time work experience (thirty-five to forty years or more) at arduous unskilled physical labor who has little education, a significant impairment that prevents him from performing his previous kind of work, and no demonstrated ability to do lighter work may be deemed incapable of substantial gainful activity and may qualify for benefits.[4]

Applicants who fail to meet either of the above tests must be evaluated in terms of a more subjective test that requires determination of how a claimant's impairments affect residual skills needed to perform many undemanding jobs available in the national economy. The amount of subjective judgment involved in weighing medical and economic data, coupled with the enormous case load, make it unlikely that state agencies or their federal overseers will ever be able to eliminate inconsistencies and inequities inherent in this test.[5]

After the state agency makes a determination for or against the claimant, his file is forwarded to the Bureau of Disability Insurance at SSA headquarters in Baltimore. This bureau has the statutory authority to reverse a recommended approval, but it cannot reverse a state denial

---

[2] Robert G. Dixon, Jr., *Social Security Disability and Mass Justice* (New York: Praeger Publishers, 1973), p. 54.

[3] Ibid., p. 55.

[4] Ibid., p. 56.

[5] Ibid., pp. 63–92; for regulations on disability, see *Code of Federal Regulations*, Title 20, Part 404.1539, appendix, pp. 349–64.

of benefits. Before 1971, this bureau reviewed all state determinations. Since 1971, the bureau has been reviewing a 5 percent sample for the purpose of monitoring state agencies. A 2 percent sample is reviewed by the bureau's medical staff for the purpose of evaluating the effectiveness of the SSA guidelines. State awards examined in these samples may be reversed, but such reversals are rare.

SSA notifies claimants of the results of the initial determination. In fiscal year 1976, benefit claims of 482,238 applicants were approved at this stage, an allowance rate of 38.1 percent. [6]

Reconsideration. If a claim is denied, the claimant has six months to file a request for reconsideration. On reconsideration, all claims are reviewed by both the state agency and the Bureau of Disability Insurance examiners. The claimant may add information to his medical file. About 30 percent (223,100) of claims initially denied were reconsidered in fiscal year 1976, with a reversal rate of 29.8 percent. Reversals may result from new information or deterioration of the claimant's condition as well as from reevaluation of the initial claim.

Hearing request. Upon denial of a reconsideration, the claimant may within six months request a hearing before an administrative law judge. The hearing is held within seventy-five miles of the claimant's home The claimant may appear in person and has a right to counsel. Government medical and vocational specialists are sometimes present. Testimony is recorded and taken under oath. Unlike the Bureau of Disability Insurance examiners, these judges have the authority to reverse state agency denials. In fiscal year 1976, SSA's administrative law judges processed 36,600 hearing requests, and they reversed denials in 47 percent of the cases. This high rate of reversal may result from introduction of new evidence or a finding of error in procedure, but it may also reflect a difference in approach between judges and the state and federal examiners responsible for initial determinations and reconsiderations. [7]

Appeals council. The final step in the nonjudicial determination process is the thirteen-member appeals council. After denial by an administrative law judge, a claimant has sixty days to request a review by this body. The appeals council has the option of denying a request for review, and most requests are denied. If the council decides to review the case, the claimant may file a written brief or appear in person in Arlington, Virginia. The council also has the authority to transfer to

---

[6] U.S. Congress, House of Representatives, Committee on Ways and Means, *Annual Report of the Social Security Administration for Fiscal Year 1976*, 95th Congress, 1st session, April 1977, p. 15.

[7] Dixon, *Social Security Disability and Mass Justice*, pp. 75–79.

itself appeals pending before an administrative law judge and to accept cases referred to it by these judges. In fiscal year 1976, the appeals council handled 1,100 cases and ruled in favor of the claimant in only 6.7 percent of them.

Court action. Once a claimant has exhausted all channels of administrative appeal, he may bring suit in a U.S. District Court within sixty days following a decision or denial of request for review by the appeals council. District court decisions are subject to appeal by the claimant or the government to a Federal Court of Appeals or the U.S. Supreme Court. In 1976, the court affirmation rate of SSA denials was 83 percent; the cumulative affirmation rate as of that year was 77 percent.

Payment of Benefits

Once DI benefits have been awarded, payments begin with the fifth full calendar month in which the claimant is disabled. Payments may be retroactive (but not for more than seventeen months before the application was filed). The waiting period is waived for a previously disabled worker returning to the DI roll. The purpose of this provision is to encourage workers on disability to return to work without facing the prospect of losing benefits for five months should they again become disabled.

DI benefits are terminated when the beneficiary dies, when he reaches age sixty-five (when DI is replaced by old age insurance), or when his medical condition improves so that he is no longer considered disabled. In the latter case, benefits terminate after three months.

If a recipient returns to gainful employment in spite of his medical impairment, benefits will be paid during a nine-month trial work period. If at that time it is determined that he is capable of substantial gainful activity, benefits are terminated after an additional three months. The nine-month trial work period is another means of encouraging workers with impairments to make an effort to return to the labor force and become self-supporting.

After twenty-four consecutive months of receiving disability benefits, recipients acquire hospital and supplementary insurance protection under medicare. Coverage remains in effect during the trial work period but ceases when benefit payments stop. A previously disabled worker returning to benefit status must again wait twenty-four months for medicare coverage. This provision has been criticized for its disincentive effect on beneficiaries who may be considering a return to the labor force.

Benefits to Disabled Widows, Widowers, and Disabled Dependent Children

A widow or widower of an insured worker who meets the other requirements for widow's or widower's benefits may be eligible for disabled widow's or widower's benefits. To qualify, an individual must have a medically determinable physical or mental impairment expected to last for not less than one year and of sufficient severity to preclude the individual from engaging in any gainful activity.[8] This test is stricter than that applied to workers and in effect limits eligibility to the first of the three tests cited above. Benefits are paid only to persons aged fifty to fifty-nine. At age sixty, they become eligible for survivor's benefits. Monthly payments are reduced slightly for each month of entitlement before age sixty.

Childhood disability benefits are payable to disabled children of a worker entitled to OASDI benefits. The criteria for disability are the same as those for covered workers. To qualify, the onset of disability must have occurred before age twenty-two.

Disability payments to widows, widowers, and disabled children are paid out of the OASI trust fund, except for disabled children of workers drawing DI benefits, who are paid from the DI fund.

The Determination Process: How Well Does It Work?

The quality of the efforts of the administrative apparatus described above has great significance for both the disabled population and taxpayers. Rapid growth in the application rate and the number of awards has fed suspicions that examiners and administrative law judges are becoming more permissive. More than 1.2 million DI claims are received each year. The difficulty of agreeing on a set of objective criteria for determining who is totally disabled is a continuing source of concern. Failure to establish consistent criteria and basing the determination on vocational factors can result in arbitrary awards of benefits and inequities among claimants. The division of labor between state agencies and SSA adds another source of potential inconsistency in the awards process.

Improving the Definition. The statute defines disability as "the inability to engage in any substantial gainful activity" because of a physical or mental impairment expected to last at least one year. It goes on to specify that a person cannot, "considering his age, education, and work experience, engage in any other kind of substantial

---

[8] *Code of Federal Regulations*, Title 20, Part 404.1504, p. 342.

16

gainful work which exists in the national economy." In many borderline cases, implementation of the statutory test can be very difficult, and objective criteria are needed. In 1960 the medical listings served as the basis for 70 percent of all benefit allowances; impairments deemed equivalent to the medical lists served as the basis for 20 percent of allowances. Vocational factors accounted for only 10 percent. Since 1960 these percentages have shown a continuous shift away from reliance on the more objective medical listings. In 1975, only 29 percent of all allowances were based on medical listings. Impairments deemed equivalent to the listings accounted for 45 percent of allowances, and vocational factors accounted for 26 percent. [9]

Evidence from two surveys indicates that concern about the objectivity and consistency of the determination process is justified. The first survey compared determinations for a sample of DI claims by agencies in three states (Louisiana, Minnesota, and Ohio) and by the Bureau of Disability Insurance examiners with determinations of the same claims by clinical teams trained in vocational rehabilitation. The test procedure began with an initial determination by a state agency. A duplicate of each file in the sample (excluding the determination decision and evidence from any medical examinations procured by state agencies) was forwarded to a clinical team composed of a social worker, a physician, an occupational therapist, and a vocational counselor. The team gathered socioeconomic, medical, psychological, and vocational information through a series of interviews, examinations, and tests; they then determined the extent of the claimant's disability. Evidence gathered by the clinical team, excluding evaluative statements, was added to the claimant's file and returned to state agencies for reevaluation and redetermination of the benefit decision. Files were then forwarded to the Bureau of Disability Insurance for final determination. Usual procedures were followed at the bureau (at the time of the survey in the late 1960s, all state agency decisions, not just a sample, were reviewed by the bureau); as in the case of redetermination at the state level, however, the files were enriched by information gathered by the clinical teams.

Since both sets of decision makers had access to essentially the same set of data, it is possible to compare the disability determinations reached under the legal procedures employed by the states and the Bureau of Disability Insurance with the determinations derived from the procedures of the clinical teams. Using the legal procedures, state

---

[9] U.S. Congress, House of Representatives, Subcommittee on Social Security of the Committee on Ways and Means, *Disability Insurance—Legislative Issue Paper*, 94th Congress, 2d session, May 1976, p. 17.

and Bureau of Disability Insurance examiners must either allow benefits, implying that the individual is totally disabled as defined in the statute and the SSA regulations, or deny benefits, implying that the individual is capable of substantial gainful employment. The clinical teams made evaluations based on an eight-point scale of work capability ranging from "fit for work under normal conditions" to "not fit for work." To facilitate comparison the eight categories were collapsed into two, those who can work full- or part-time and those who cannot work competitively.

The aggregate results using the two approaches appear to be reasonably consistent. The state-SSA examiners awarded benefits to 61.5 percent of the claimants in the sample, whereas the clinical teams found 68 percent unable to work competitively. The clinical teams concluded that 19 percent of those allowed DI benefits could work at least part-time. The clinical teams concluded that 48 percent of those denied benefits could not work competitively. The two decision processes appear to be most inconsistent in this latter category.

Several points are noteworthy in interpreting these results. The clinical teams had personal contact with claimants; in keeping with standard practice, the state and Bureau of Disability Insurance examiners had access only to written files. Beyond the initial determination by the state agencies, both groups had access to more information than is typically available to claimants' files. Although there may be a presumption that the clinical teams are more likely to make a correct evaluation, this cannot be proved. What is clear is that the legal and clinical approaches led to different results in 30 percent of the cases, thereby highlighting the fact that there are ambiguities in the determination process. The survey director, Saad Z. Nagi, attributes the different results partly to differences in criteria used and partly to differences in training.[10]

A more recent survey, conducted by the General Accounting Office, was designed to check for consistency in the way agencies in different states decide claims. In fiscal year 1975 state agencies denied benefits to 50 percent of the claims at the stage of initial determination. The percentage denied ranged from 34 percent in Iowa to 62 percent in New Mexico. Again, these differences are not proof of inconsistency, since the composition of disability applicants may differ substantially among states.

The General Accounting Office checked for consistency by drawing a random sample of 221 claims for disability under social security

---

[10] Saad Z. Nagi, *Disability and Rehabilitation* (Columbus: Ohio State University Press, 1969), p. 93.

or the Supplemental Security Income (SSI) program after they had been decided in the state of origin. Copies of the files were sent to state agencies in ten other states and to Bureau of Disability Insurance examiners in Baltimore. In only 38 of the cases (32 approvals and 6 denials) did all ten states and the Bureau of Disability Insurance concur in the initial determination made by the state of origin. In 10 cases, the bureau and all ten states agreed that more information was needed before a decision could be made. In the remaining 173 cases (78 percent), there was less than complete agreement on whether the claim should be approved or denied. The General Accounting Office also noted that, in many of the 156 cases in which a majority of the states agreed, they disagreed on the rationale of the decision.[11]

To improve disability determination procedures, SSA is introducing a set of vocational regulations as a supplement to the list of medical impairments. The new regulations relate degrees of impairment expressed in terms of ability to perform different kinds of work—such as heavy, light, and sedentary—to nonmedical factors such as age, education, and work experience. They represent an attempt to add specific, objective, nonmedical standards to the medical standards used in determining disability.

Once the new regulations go into effect, they are expected to promote greater uniformity in decisions of state agencies and the Bureau of Disability Insurance. They will be made binding on administrative law judges in an apparent attempt to reduce the current high rate of reversals. Finally, the new regulations will provide information to the public so that claimants and their representatives will be better informed about the criteria on which decisions are based. Only after a period of careful monitoring will it be possible to determine whether the new regulations are working.

Administrative Performance. The administrative apparatus that has been created to handle the massive disability case loads may be partly responsible for the rapid increase in claims and awards. Some conjectural evidence can be offered to support this view.

In 1969, Congress passed legislation providing benefits for coal miners who are victims of black lung, and for several years the Bureau of Disability Insurance determined eligibility from evidence gathered by state agencies. Then, in 1972, legislation created the Supplemental Security Income program, which federalized categorical public assistance for the aged, blind, and permanently and totally disabled. Persons

---

[11] House of Representatives, Subcommittee on Social Security, *Disability Insurance—Legislative Issue Paper*, p. 10.

applying for SSI benefits since January 1, 1974, are required to meet the same criteria for disability or blindness as recipients of DI, and their applications are processed through the same state-federal administrative channels. SSI applicants are often automatically screened for DI eligibility. SSI generated a sudden and massive increase in workload and in the backlog of undecided cases. By 1974, the workload included nearly 1 million SSI disability cases and about 500,000 black lung cases in addition to the 1.2 million claims for DI.

Federal administrators, claimants, and members of Congress began to apply pressure to speed up the determination process. Examiners were encouraged to increase their case-load productivity. According to information gathered by the staff of the Subcommittee on Social Security of the House Ways and Means Committee, one consequence of the emphasis on case production was to de-emphasize medical and vocational documentation.[12] At the same time, state agencies were forced to double the size of their staffs. A number of state agencies reported a tendency for new employees with limited training to be more liberal in awarding benefits.[13] The staff buildups occurred after federal review of state decisions was relaxed when the Bureau of Disability Insurance began reviewing only a small sample of cases.

An examination of the raw data on state agency denials does not appear to support the contention that the award process has been liberalized. Over the past decade, the state denial rate has risen from less than 40 percent to about 50 percent. The higher denial rate is consistent with a relaxation of standards, however, if it can be demonstrated that such factors as labor market conditions, higher benefit levels, public awareness of the program, and changing attitudes toward work are encouraging more borderline applicants to apply for benefits. Evidence presented in the following chapter will show that this seems to be happening.

---

[12] Ibid., p. 5.

[13] Ibid.

4

The Effect of Disability on Labor Force Participation and Earnings

The ability to work is obviously affected by the state of one's health. The effect of health on labor force participation and earnings is a result of the interaction of a worker's physical condition, job requirements, and behavioral response.

An important source of information about the health and disability status of working-age adults is the 1972 Survey of Disabled and Nondisabled Adults. The survey collected and detailed information from a sample of the 106 million adults aged twenty to sixty-four who constituted the civilian, noninstitutionalized population.[1] Survey results indicate that 52 million adults, or nearly half of all working-age adults, report some form of chronic health problem or impairment.

Respondents with impairments lasting three months or longer were asked if they fell into any of these three categories:

- Severely disabled—unable to work altogether or unable to work regularly;

- Occupationally disabled—able to work regularly, but not at the occupation in which one worked before onset; or

- Limited to secondary work—able to work full-time at the same occupation but with limitations on the kind or amount of work.

Women who were customarily not employed or who had never worked and whose condition precluded them from keeping house were also classified as severely disabled.

Survey results indicate that 15.5 million adults, or about 14 percent of the adult working-age population, fell into one of the above

---

[1] For a description of the survey, see Kathryn H. Allen, "First Findings of the 1972 Survey of the Disabled: General Characteristics," *Social Security Bulletin*, vol. 39, no. 10 (October 1976), pp. 18–37.

categories, and that 7.7 million, or 7 percent, were severely disabled. Applications for disability insurance can be expected to originate from the latter group. Among the 7.7 million severely disabled, only an estimated 1.5 million, or 19 percent, received DI benefits. An additional 1.0 million received some form of public assistance. [2]

Several reasons can be cited for the difference between the number of severely disabled and the number receiving DI benefits. The survey definition of severe disability was based on the respondent's assessment of the effect of an impairment on the ability to work, whereas eligibility for benefits is based primarily on clinical evidence prescribed in SSA regulations. Many who regard themselves as severely disabled are denied benefits. Also, because of the SSA requirements of previous labor force attachment, many working-age adults are not eligible. The Social Security Administration estimates that in 1972 less than three-fourths of the population aged twenty to sixty-four met the work-history requirements for DI coverage. [3]

The importance of prior labor force attachment is illustrated by comparing DI recipients with disabled recipients of public assistance. According to the survey, the estimated 1 million severely disabled persons receiving either aid to the permanently and totally disabled or aid to the blind amounted to about 43 percent of the total number of persons receiving public assistance. In most states, the definition of disability under these programs was similar to the definition under DI. Other disabled needy persons received Aid to Families with Dependent Children (AFDC), general assistance, or some combination of the above. [4]

Table 5 shows the extent to which prior labor force attachment is related to eligibility for DI. In 1972, over two-thirds of the DI recipients were male. This is probably because male workers are typically in the work force for more years than female workers and are more likely to have had recent work experience, as indicated by their higher rate of employment at onset. Table 5 shows that a larger percentage of men receiving DI than of women were employed at onset and had been employed for more than ten years.

Another factor keeping severely disabled persons off the DI rolls appears to be a lack of knowledge about the program. An estimated 206,000 severely disabled persons receiving public assistance payments in 1972 had sufficient labor force attachment to qualify for DI.

[2] Michael Hooker and Aaron Krute, "Disabled-Worker Beneficiaries Under OASDI: Comparison with Severely Disabled PA Recipients," *Social Security Bulletin*, vol. 40, no. 8 (August 1977), p. 17.

[3] *Social Security Bulletin*, Annual Statistical Supplement (1975), p. 82.

[4] Hooker and Krute, "Disabled-Worker Beneficiaries Under OASDI," p. 16.

TABLE 5

LABOR FORCE ATTACHMENT OF SEVERELY DISABLED RECIPIENTS OF
DISABILITY INSURANCE AND PUBLIC ASSISTANCE, 1972
(percentage distribution)

Labor Force Participation	Disabled-Worker Beneficiaries			Public Assistance Recipients		
	Total	Men	Women	Total	Men	Women
Total number in labor force (thousands)	1,489	1,071	418	1,003	286	717
Employment status at onset						
Employed	87.3	90.6	78.7	43.6	59.6	37.2
Not employed	12.7	9.3	21.2	56.4	40.3	62.8
Duration of employment before onset						
Less than 1 year	9.7	10.2	8.2	36.3	33.0	37.6
1 to 10 years	49.5	46.4	57.8	37.0	33.6	38.4
More than 10 years	39.8	42.4	33.2	15.1	31.1	8.4
Not reported	1.0	1.1	0.8	11.7	2.3	15.7

SOURCE: Michael Hooker and Aaron Krute, "Disabled-Worker Beneficiaries Under OASDI: Comparison with Severely Disabled PA Recipients," *Social Security Bulletin*, vol. 40, no. 8 (August 1977), p. 17.

Of this group, 60 percent said they did not apply for DI benefits because they did not know about them, and 35 percent said they were unaware of their own eligibility. It is not clear whether this was due to a misunderstanding about eligibility requirements or to a feeling that their disability was not severe enough.[5] Severely disabled applicants for SSI and for DI are now processed through the same channels. Since the definition of disability is the same under both programs, ignorance of the DI program is less likely to be a factor now than it was in 1972.

A reason why some persons do not receive disability benefits of any kind is that recipients of both DI and SSI face rather strict limits on earnings from labor as a condition for eligibility. Severely disabled persons who can work probably weigh the level of benefits they might receive from DI or SSI against the income they could earn if they continued to work. Forgone potential earnings become an opportu-

[5] Ibid., p. 19.

TABLE 6

CHANGE IN WORK STATUS FOR SEVERELY DISABLED ADULT POPULATION
AGED TWENTY TO SIXTY-FOUR EMPLOYED BEFORE ONSET, 1972

| | | Percentage Distribution by Work Status | | |
| | | | Work reduced | |
Age (at survey)	Number (thousands)	No change	Still working	Not working
Under 34	339	17.5	9.2	73.3
35–44	595	23.4	11.5	65.1
45–54	1,258	10.1	7.4	82.5
55–64	2,281	8.3	5.7	86.0

SOURCE: Evan S. Schechter, "Employment and Work Adjustment of the Disabled: 1972 Survey of Disabled and Nondisabled Adults," *Social Security Bulletin*, vol. 40, no. 7 (July 1977), p. 5.

nity cost for those who receive benefits that are conditioned on earnings limits, and the level of potential earnings becomes an important variable in the decision process of potential applicants.

Econometric Studies

Disability undoubtedly reduces labor force participation and lowers the earnings of workers. Lower earnings occur because workers are often required to reduce hours of work or to drop out of the labor force completely. Also, limitations on performance may force workers to seek less demanding jobs at lower pay. Data from the 1972 Survey of Disabled and Nondisabled Adults, shown in Table 6, show the extent to which severe disability altered the work status of respondents who were employed before they became disabled. Only in the age bracket of those thirty-five to forty-four are more than 20 percent of the severely disabled working full-time, and even in that age group 65 percent have stopped working altogether. Work reduction is particularly great for older workers and women.[6]

The negative effect of poor health on labor supply and earnings is documented in several econometric studies. Two different approaches have been used to separate the effect of health from the effects of other determinants of labor force behavior. In one approach, separate equations for subsamples of working-age adults with and

[6] Evan S. Schechter, "Employment and Work Adjustment of the Disabled: 1972 Survey of Disabled and Nondisabled Adults," *Social Security Bulletin*, vol. 40, no. 7 (July 1977), p. 5. Because of the phrasing of the questionnaire, the relationship between severe disability and reduced work effort may come close to being tautological.

without health problems are used. By comparing the two sets of estimates, the effect of ill health on labor supply and earnings can be isolated. In the second approach, health variables are added to standard labor supply equations. Effects of health are then determined by comparing the explanatory power of equations with and without health variables and by analyzing the value and significance of health variable coefficients.

Comparisons of "Well" and "Sick" Adults. Harold S. Luft has estimated the effect of health on labor force participation, weeks worked, unemployment, and various measures of earning capacity by comparing persons who are well with those who are sick.[7] He used data from the 1967 Survey of Economic Opportunity, a detailed source of socioeconomic and demographic information collected from a sample of adults aged eighteen to sixty-four. The well subsample consisted of those who reported no health condition affecting their ability to work. The sick subsample included those reporting a health condition that either prevented them from working or limited in some way the kind or amount of work they could perform.[8] The well and sick subsamples were each divided into four groups according to race (black and white) and sex. There are usually significant differences in labor market behavior among races and sexes.

Although one way to measure the effect of health on labor supply and earnings is to compare averages of the well and sick subsamples, this can be misleading and is rejected by Luft. If other characteristics of well and sick individuals were not identical, the observed differences would not measure the true health effects. As might be expected, the socioeconomic and demographic characteristics of the two groups are different. In particular, disability is more common among older workers and among those with less education.

The "true" effect of ill health can be measured by comparing the observed status of the sick with what their status would be if they were well. Since the latter cannot be observed, it must be estimated. Luft chose to estimate the presumed "well" status of the sick by fitting a standard labor supply regression equation to the subsample of well respondents in each of the four race-sex groups. Separate equations were estimated for nine labor supply and earnings variables. The independent variables—that is, the variables thought to

---

[7] Harold S. Luft, "The Impact of Poor Health on Earnings," *Review of Economics and Statistics*, vol. 57, no. 1 (February 1975), pp. 43–57.

[8] Recent evidence indicates that poor health contributes to high absentee rates among employed workers. See Steven Glen Allen, "Absenteeism and the Labor Market" (Ph.D. diss., Harvard University, May 1978), pp. 112–13.

TABLE 7

EFFECT OF ILL HEALTH ON LABOR SUPPLY AND EARNINGS OF ADULTS
AGED EIGHTEEN TO SIXTY-FOUR

Race, Sex, and Health Status	Percent Who Worked Last Week[a] (1)	Labor Force Experience Preceding Year (1966)				
		Percent in labor force (2)	Weeks worked (3)	Hours worked per week (4)	Hourly wage (dollars) (5)	Annual earnings (dollars) (6)
White men						
Estimated average if well	84.48	96.29	46.72	43.19	3.08	6,174
Observed average if sick	63.25	78.54	42.33	41.61	2.70	4,758
Change owing to ill health	−21.23	−17.75	−4.39	−1.58	−0.38	−1,416
Percentage difference	25.13	18.43	10.55	3.66	12.34	22.93
Black men						
Estimated average if well	80.89	94.89	45.39	40.18	2.15	3,853
Observed average if sick	46.04	67.97	38.24	35.73	1.91	2,843
Change owing to ill health	−34.85	−26.92	−7.15	−4.45	−0.24	−1,010
Percentage difference	43.08	28.37	15.75	11.08	11.16	26.21
White women						
Estimated average if well	45.61	58.60	40.37	36.56	2.03	2,654
Observed average if sick	23.22	40.63	32.21	33.04	1.82	1,703
Change owing to ill health	−22.39	−17.97	−8.16	−3.52	−0.21	−951
Percentage difference	49.09	30.67	20.21	10.65	10.34	35.83
Black women						
Estimated average if well	55.30	72.59	38.13	33.64	1.30	1,521
Observed average if sick	26.70	50.88	30.40	28.18	1.36	1,040

TABLE 7 (Continued)

Race, Sex, and Health Status	Percent Who Worked Last Week[a] (1)	Labor Force Experience Preceding Year (1966)				
		Percent in labor force (2)	Weeks worked (3)	Hours worked per week (4)	Hourly wage (dollars) (5)	Annual earnings (dollars) (6)
Change owing to ill health	−28.60	−21.71	−7.73	−5.46	0.06	−481
Percentage difference	51.76	29.91	20.27	16.23	−4.62	31.62

[a] Refers to week before week of survey interview. Survey was taken in 1967.
SOURCE: Harold S. Luft, "Impact of Poor Health on Earnings," *Review of Economics and Statistics*, vol. 57, no. 1 (February 1975), p. 46.

determine or explain labor supply and earnings—include age, education, family structure, earnings of other family members, and region of residence.

Luft first derived the regression coefficients from data in the well subsample. He then inserted the observed values of independent variables from the sick subsample into these equations. In this way, he obtained an estimate of how the sick would have behaved had they been well. His procedure is based on the assumption that those in the sick subsample would have behaved like those in the well sample if they were not sick. There is no apparent reason why this should not be the case. By comparing the observed labor supply and earnings averages for persons in the sick subsample with an estimate of what the averages would have been if the same persons would have been well, Luft obtained an estimate of the "true" effect of ill health on labor market performance.

A summary of some of Luft's results is shown in Table 7. All race and sex groupings experience sizable reductions in amount of work and earnings as a result of ill health. The first column shows the effect of health problems on the percentage who worked during the week before they were sampled. Ill health is associated with a drop of from 25 percent for white men to about 50 percent for women of both races. Columns 2 through 6 are for 1966, the year preceding the survey. Column 2 shows a decline in labor force participation of about 18 percent for white men and roughly 30 percent for women and black men.

Columns 3 through 6 apply only to those who continued to work at least part-time in 1966. The average number of weeks worked per year and hours worked per week are lower for workers with health limitations, with greater reductions for women and black men than for white men. Health problems are likely to reduce labor productivity and, hence, to reduce wages. Luft's estimates show a reduction of 10 to 12 percent in hourly wages, except for black women. As a result of the lower wages and fewer hours worked, annual earnings fall. The earnings drop in dollars is greatest for white men, but in percentage terms the reduction is greatest for white women.

Estimates of the Importance of Health in General Labor Supply Equations. The second approach to measuring the effect of health variables on labor force behavior is found in studies by Scheffler and Iden and by Berkowitz, Johnson, and Murphy.[9] Many studies of labor supply have found age, sex, race, education, and family status and size to be significant determinants of labor force behavior. In determining the labor supply of an individual, actual or potential wage rates and family income from other sources are also important. Both the Scheffler-Iden and the Berkowitz-Johnson-Murphy studies use measures of these variables as independent variables in their labor supply equations. In addition, both studies follow the common two-stage approach by estimating separate equations for labor force participation and for hours or weeks worked.

The participation decision involves the choice between (1) not working and (2) working or seeking work (and thereby becoming a participant in the labor force). Once a worker decides to participate, he must then decide how many hours per week and how many weeks per year to work. Institutional constraints such as involuntary unemployment and the forty-hour week limit the options of many workers, but varying degrees of flexibility are possible by choosing part-time work, accepting or refusing overtime, or holding more than one job.

Scheffler and Iden, like Luft, used data from the 1967 Survey of Economic Opportunity. They estimated separate labor force participation and labor supply equations for black and white males aged twenty-five to fifty-four and aged fifty-five to sixty-four. When health variables indicating presence of a primary or a secondary impairment and duration of an impairment were added, the explanatory value

[9] Richard M. Scheffler and George Iden, "The Effect of Disability on Labor Supply," *Industrial and Labor Relations Review*, vol. 28, no. 1 (October 1974), pp. 122–32; Monroe Berkowitz, William G. Johnson, and Edward H. Murphy, *Public Policy Toward Disability* (New York: Praeger Publishers, 1976).

of the labor force participation equations increased substantially for all four age-race groupings. [10] Coefficients of the health variables were negative, indicating that the presence and duration of impairments reduce labor force participation. All coefficients were significant at the 1 percent level for black and white males aged twenty-five to fifty-four; coefficients were negative, and all but one were significant at least at the 10 percent level for males aged fifty-five to sixty-four.

Results were somewhat less conclusive when health status variables were added to equations for estimating hours or weeks worked. In most cases, the health variables significantly improved the explanatory value; in nearly all cases, the coefficients of the impairment variables indicated that, for males who did participate in the labor market, the presence of impairments reduced the supply of labor. A somewhat surprising result was the apparent positive relationship between duration of impairments and supply of effort. Scheffler-Iden indicate that this might result from successful efforts at rehabilitation. [11]

The Berkowitz-Johnson-Murphy study is similar in approach, but it uses data from the 1966 social security Survey of Disabled Adults. The authors are able to draw inferences only about labor force behavior of persons with impairments, because persons without some type of impairment limiting their capacity to work were not included in the 1966 survey. [12] Participation and labor supply equations were estimated for black and white males aged twenty-five to fifty-four and fifty-five to sixty-four. Variables measuring nine types of functional or mental limitations on ability to work were added to equations for labor force participation and, for those who worked, hours worked during 1965. Respondents receiving DI, Aid to the Permanently and Totally Disabled, and Aid to the Blind were excluded from the data set because generally they are required not to work as a condition of eligibility for benefits. Because the authors wanted to measure the relationship between transfers and labor force activity, inclusion in the sample of persons who had to cease working to qualify for benefits would bias the estimate of the coefficient of the transfer variable. This decision removed many of the most severely disabled from the sample.

Although the Berkowitz-Johnson-Murphy results are based on a smaller and more restrictive sample, they are quite similar to those

[10] Scheffler and Iden, "Effect of Disability on Labor Supply," pp. 126–27.
[11] Ibid., p. 132.
[12] The 1966 Survey of Disabled Adults sampled 8,700 adults aged sixteen to sixty-four. This was a sample representative of an estimated 17.8 million working-age adults with disabilities in 1966.

of Scheffler-Iden. The addition of health variables to participation and labor supply equations generally increases their explanatory power, in some cases substantially.[13] The evidence on the effect of specific limitations on participation and hours worked is less conclusive, but this is largely because of the nature of the sample. Since all respondents reported at least one impairment, and since those receiving work-conditioned public transfers are excluded, it is difficult to anticipate the direction or magnitude of the effect of any one impairment on labor force behavior.

Implications of the Effects of Disability

The econometric studies confirm the expectation that people with physical or mental impairments tend to work less and earn lower wages than people in otherwise similar circumstances who are healthy. To the extent that they suffer from disabilities that reduce their labor productivity, their potential wage rate is likely to fall. Lower wages in turn lower the opportunity cost of not working or of working less. In many cases, disability makes work more inconvenient and, in some cases, physically painful.

Lower wage rates reduce the opportunity cost of alternative uses of time, encouraging disabled workers to work less, but lower wages also reduce income, and that encourages people to work more. If disabled workers can recoup most or all of their income losses from not working by qualifying for DI or some other public transfer, the economic incentive to continue working may be weakened considerably. Since a disabled person who leaves the labor force and qualifies for DI is relieved of income and payroll taxes on earnings as well as the costs of holding a job, benefit payments well below gross earnings may become an attractive alternative.

The incentive to apply for DI is strengthened if working is inconvenient or painful. Lack of employment opportunities may also encourage disabled workers to apply, and the Luft study cited above indicates that unemployment rates are about twice as high for those in the sick subsample after adjusting for differences in other characteristics.[14]

For individuals who are members of a family unit, the lower earnings and potential disability benefits resulting from the disability of one member may encourage a shift in labor force participation among family members. The disabled member may withdraw and be

---

[13] Berkowitz, Johnson, and Murphy, *Public Policy Toward Disability*, p. 89.
[14] Luft, "Impact of Poor Health on Earnings," p. 46.

replaced as a wage earner by a spouse or other family members of working age. This type of shift is particularly attractive to workers who qualify for DI benefits, because eligibility is contingent on absence of significant labor market activity by the recipient but is totally unaffected by other sources of family income.

5

The Level of Disability Benefits and the Recipients

Social security disability benefits are calculated in much the same way as retirement and survivors benefits. Benefits are based on the taxable earnings of the worker during past periods of covered employment. The Social Security Amendments of 1977 substantially changed the method of calculating monthly payments; these changes apply to all disability awards after January 1, 1979. For other social security benefits—retirement and survivors—the new method is to be phased in over a five-year period beginning in 1979. The new method of calculating benefits has important implications for future DI recipients, because it redresses the former tendency to discriminate in favor of younger disabled workers.

How Benefits Are Calculated

Under the old law, benefits for each applicant were based on average monthly earnings (AME) in covered employment. To calculate the AME, the total taxable earnings of the worker are determined for each year beginning with 1951 or the year after the worker reached age twenty-one, whichever is later. The five years with the lowest earnings are dropped (subject to the constraint that at least two years remain). Taxed earnings in the remaining years, referred to as the benefit computation years, are summed to get covered income. This sum is divided by the number of months in the benefit computation years to obtain the AME.

For example, the AME for a worker who reached age twenty-one in 1964 and became disabled in 1978 equals his total taxed earnings divided by ninety-six months. Thirteen years have elapsed since 1965, the year after the worker turned twenty-one. Dropping the five years of lowest covered earnings, the benefit computation period is eight years or ninety-six months. Under the disability "freeze" provision, any years in which the worker was declared disabled during the intervening period may also be dropped from the computation. Because covered earnings are likely to be low or nonexistent during disability, dropping these years raises the AME.

A benefit formula is applied to the AME to determine the basic monthly benefit, or primary insurance amount (PIA). Although benefits in dollar terms are positively related to the AME, the benefit formula contains a redistributive element that yields a PIA that is a higher percentage of low than of high AMEs. Once benefits are awarded, they increase periodically with increases in the Consumer Price Index.

In addition to receiving the PIA, DI recipients with dependents may qualify for family benefits. Recipients with a spouse aged sixty-five or older may receive a spouse's benefit equal to 50 percent of the PIA. These benefits are paid only if they exceed the amount payable on the spouse's own account. As with retirement benefits, there is also an option to receive actuarially reduced spouses's benefits at age sixty-two. A younger spouse is eligible for a wife's benefit if she has in her care one or more dependent children under age eighteen. Children's benefits are payable for dependent children under age eighteen (or under age twenty-two for unmarried dependent children who are full-time students). Wife's and children's benefits are also set at 50 percent of PIA, but the total amount of benefits received by a family is limited by the family maximum benefit allowance. Under the law in effect before 1979, the family maximum benefit ranged from 150 percent to 188 percent of the PIA.[1] Without such a limit, many younger workers who qualify for DI benefits would receive amounts in excess of their potential earnings in the labor force. Even with the limit, benefits sometimes exceed previous earnings, particularly for low-wage workers with dependents.[2]

The new method of calculating DI benefits after January 1, 1979, was introduced as part of a new procedure for indexing benefits to inflation. Its main feature is that benefits are based on a worker's average indexed monthly earnings (AIME) rather than his average monthly earnings (AME). Wages are indexed by multiplying the ac-

---

[1] If the wife works, her benefit is subject to an earnings offset identical to the retirement test for workers eligible for retirement benefits. In 1979, benefits are reduced 50 cents for each dollar of earnings in excess of $4,500.

[2] A sample of workers awarded DI benefits in October 1976 shows that in a few cases, particularly among workers in the lowest earnings categories, workers received benefits well in excess of previous average earnings. See Francisco R. Bayo and Joseph F. Faber, "Actual Replacement Rates for Disabled Worker Beneficiaries," *Actuarial Note No. 94* (Social Security Administration, January 1978), Table 1.

tual covered earnings of each past year by the ratio of the average covered wages of all workers two years before that in which the worker became disabled to average covered wages in the year the wage was earned.[3] For example, assume that a worker had earned $4,000 in 1961 and became disabled in 1979. The second year before he became disabled was 1977. In that year, the average wage in covered employment was 2.393 times that of 1961. The amount used for 1961 in determining his benefits is $9,572—the $4,000 he earned in 1961 multiplied by 2.393. The earnings of each year are indexed in this same way.

Average wages in covered employment have risen substantially since the early 1950s because of the combined effects of inflation and increases in labor productivity, and the upper limit on earnings subject to the payroll tax has increased in sizable jumps, especially since the mid-1960s. As a result, the AME of most workers with long work histories—unadjusted for changes in average wages—was held down by low taxable earnings in early years. When earnings are indexed, the low earnings of earlier years are adjusted upward, and discrimination against workers with long work histories is eliminated.

Aside from indexing covered wages, no changes have been made in the procedure for calculating a worker's PIA. Total indexed earnings in covered employment are summed, the five lowest years are dropped, and the AIME is determined by dividing the indexed total by the number of months in the benefit computation years. Because a worker's AIME is generally much larger than his unindexed AME, the benefit formula has been changed by reducing the percentages of the AIME allowed in calculating the benefit. As in the previous law, the new benefit formula is redistributive, in that the PIA is a higher percentage of low than of high AIMEs.

Under the new law, the amount of the family maximum benefit for 1979 increases from 150 percent of the PIA (for PIAs up to $230) up to 188 percent of the PIA (at $332) and then declines to 175 percent of the PIA (above $433). The new law also established a new minimum benefit of $121 per month. The family maximum will increase as wages increase, but the minimum will remain at the 1979 level.

Effects of the 1977 Amendments

The principal objective of the new procedure for indexing social security benefits was to correct the overindexing of benefits resulting

---

[3] For a discussion of the new indexing technique, see Colin D. Campbell, *The 1977 Amendments to the Social Security Act* (Washington, D.C.: American Enterprise Institute, 1978), pp. 11–15.

TABLE 8

PRIMARY INSURANCE AMOUNTS UNDER DISABILITY INSURANCE FOR
SELECTED EARNINGS RECORDS
(dollars)

Elapsed Years of Covered Employment	Employed Full-Time at Minimum Wage		Earnings at or above Taxable Maximum	
	Old law (1)	New law (2)	Old law (3)	New law (4)
1951–1978	236.40	242.70	456.40	454.90
1965–1978	275.80	243.60	556.20	480.60
1977–1978	320.20	236.30	642.90	502.60

NOTE: Old law refers to provisions before the 1977 amendments to the Social Security Act. Calculations are based on the formula in use beginning June 1977. New law refers to provisions in the 1977 amendments. Calculations are based on preliminary wage indexes and may differ slightly from actual amounts.

from the 1972 amendments to the Social Security Act. In addition, the new indexing technique is significant for disability insurance because it reduces the discrimination that formerly existed against older persons with many years of covered earnings.

Table 8 gives examples of disability benefits for old and young workers under the old and the new benefit formulas. In columns 1 and 2, it is assumed that the worker was employed full-time (forty hours a week, fifty weeks a year) at the prevailing federal minimum wage and became disabled in January 1979. Under the old law, if the worker was age twenty-one or older before 1951 and worked regularly from 1951 through December 1978, his PIA would be $236.40. If a worker reached age twenty-one in 1964, worked from 1965 to 1978, and became disabled in January 1979, he would receive a PIA of $275.80. If a worker reached age twenty-one in 1977, worked full-time at the minimum wage for only two years, and became disabled in January 1979, he would have a PIA of $320.20. Under the special provision for workers under age thirty-one, such a worker would meet the requirements for minimum labor force attachment (six quarters of coverage in this example) and would qualify for benefits.[4]

Table 9 shows the differences in the replacement ratios for young and old workers, based on the data in Table 8. Replacement ratios measure the ratio of a worker's PIA to his monthly income. Under

---

[4] A worker under age thirty-one qualifies for benefits if he has worked in covered employment in one-half of the quarters that have elapsed between age twenty-one and onset, with a minimum of six quarters.

TABLE 9

REPLACEMENT RATIOS FOR DISABILITY INSURANCE RECIPIENTS RECEIVING
PRIMARY INSURANCE AMOUNTS FOR SELECTED EARNINGS RECORDS
(percent)

Elapsed Years of Covered Employment	Employed Full-Time at Minimum Wage		Earnings at or above Taxable Maximum	
	Old law	New law	Old law	New law
1951–1978	53.5	55.0	30.9	30.8
1965–1978	62.4	55.2	37.7	32.6
1977–1978	72.5	53.5	43.6	34.1

NOTE: See note to Table 8 for explanation of the headings.

the old law, a worker who worked full-time at the minimum wage from 1951 to 1978 would have received monthly DI benefits equal to 53.5 percent of his monthly earnings during his last month of employment. The replacement ratio rises to 62.4 percent for the person working from 1965 to 1978 and to 72.5 percent for the young worker qualifying for DI after two years of work. When one considers the expenses of holding a job, including payroll taxes, along with the inconvenience and possible discomfort of working, it is apparent that under the old law the young, low-wage worker had a very strong incentive to leave the labor force because of disability.

For workers with earnings at or above the maximum taxable wage, disability benefits under the old law were also highly sensitive to work history. A worker in this category from 1951 to 1978 would, on becoming disabled in January 1979, have a PIA of $456.40, as shown in column 3 of Table 8. In contrast, a young worker qualifying for DI after two years of earnings at or above the limit would have a PIA of $642.90. Table 9 shows that replacement ratios for this category of worker ranged from 30.9 percent to 43.6 percent. These ratios are below the ratios for workers with low earnings because of the redistributive nature of the benefit formula. This would cause the work disincentive effect to be weaker for workers with high earnings than for those with low earnings.

Tables 8 and 9 show that the new indexing procedure practically eliminates the difference in disability benefits for young and older workers. For persons working full-time at the federal minimum wage, the PIA is nearly independent of work history. The slightly lower benefit for the young worker with two years of covered earnings before disability is an anomaly that reflects the relatively low level of

TABLE 10

FAMILY MAXIMUM BENEFIT ALLOWANCE (FMBA) AND REPLACEMENT
RATIOS UNDER DISABILITY INSURANCE FOR SELECTED EARNINGS RECORDS

Elapsed Years of Covered Employment	Employed Full-Time at Minimum Wage		Earnings at or above Taxable Maximum	
	FMBA (dollars)	Replacement rate[a] (percent)	FMBA (dollars)	Replacement rate[b] (percent)
1951–1978	379.60	85.9	796.10	54.0
1965–1978	382.00	86.5	841.10	57.0
1977–1978	362.20	82.0	879.60	59.6

[a] Replacement rate equals family maximum benefit allowance divided by average monthly earnings at minimum wage (forty hours per week, fifty weeks per year), or $441.67 in 1978.
[b] Replacement rate equals family maximum benefit amount divided by average monthly earnings at taxable maximum, or $1,475 in 1978.

the minimum wage in real terms in 1977. The new law reduces but does not eliminate the discrepancy in replacement ratios between younger and older workers with earnings at or above the maximum taxable wage. Even with the indexing of wages, the AIME of younger workers is higher because of the rapid rise in the taxable maximum since 1973. The number of young disability claimants in this category will probably be small.

Although the lowering of the PIA and replacement ratio for young workers dampens the disincentive effect of the DI program, disincentives are still very strong for low-wage workers who are eligible for family benefits. Monthly benefits and replacement ratios for workers entitled to the family maximum benefit allowance are shown in Table 10. The examples are based on the same assumptions as in Tables 8 and 9. Since a married male worker with one dependent child in his wife's care would qualify for the maximum benefit, monthly benefits at the levels shown are common, especially for young heads of families. A family head working full-time at the federal minimum wage would receive benefits equal to about 85 percent of his earnings. When payroll taxes and expenses of working are considered, such workers have little or no economic incentive to work even under the new law if they can qualify for DI benefits. For workers earning the 1978 maximum taxable wage of $17,700 per year, the family maximum ranged from about 54 to 60 percent of gross earnings. Since workers in this category are generally subject to federal

37

and state income taxes as well as the payroll tax, they have a strong incentive to apply for DI if they are disabled.

Who Applies for Disability Insurance?

In recent years, about 1.2 million working-age adults have applied for DI benefits each year. In some cases, claimants may be physically unable to work. In other cases, applicants with a residual capacity to work are responding to economic incentives to switch to the benefit rolls. Some information is available on the socioeconomic and medical status of individual applicants. In addition, studies of the cyclical pattern of applications show a relationship between the aggregate demand for labor and the tendency to seek benefits. All of the published results draw on data from the late 1960s and early 1970s, but they should nevertheless offer some insights into the factors that motivate individuals to apply for benefits.

Age, Race, and Sex. The percentage of insured workers who apply for benefits increases with age, particularly after age fifty. This is to be expected because of the higher incidence of disabling ailments among older persons coupled with the tendency of many chronic impairments to worsen with age. A study by Mordechai E. Lando of a sample of 1971 applicants shows that for males the number of applications per 100,000 insured workers rises from 293 for those under age thirty to 4,949 for workers aged sixty to sixty-four. The rate for women ranges from 122 per 100,000 insured workers below age thirty to 3,651 per 100,000 aged sixty to sixty-four.[5] The application rate for each sex and age group is shown in Table 11.

The Lando study also presents data on application rates by race. Lando's results, summarized in Table 12, show a substantially higher claim ratio among blacks than among whites.[6] For male workers under age fifty-five, the application rate for blacks is more than twice that of whites. Overall, the application rate among black males is 1.7 times the rate for whites. Among females, the racial difference is greatest in the older age groups. For women aged fifty-five to sixty-four, the application rate for blacks is 1.8 times the rate for whites; overall, the rate for blacks is 1.5 times that for whites.

Lando speculates that the higher application rate for blacks may be attributable to a higher incidence of disability and to a lower opportunity

[5] Mordechai E. Lando, "Demographic Characteristics of Disability Applicants: Relationship to Allowances," *Social Security Bulletin,* vol. 39, no. 5 (May 1976), p. 20.
[6] Ibid.

TABLE 11

APPLICATIONS PER 100,000 WORKERS INSURED FOR DISABILITY,
BY AGE AND SEX, 1971

Age	Men	Women
Under 30	293	122
30–39	546	480
40–44	850	768
45–49	1,233	1,130
50–54	1,789	1,723
55–59	2,731	2,677
60–64	4,949	3,881
Total	1,083	949

SOURCE: Mordechai E. Lando, "Demographic Characteristics of Disability Applicants: Relationship to Allowances," *Social Security Bulletin*, vol. 39, no. 5 (May 1976), p. 20.

cost of withdrawal from the labor force. He cites evidence that blacks are more likely to suffer from impairments.[7] To the extent that blacks are more likely than whites to work as manual laborers, the impairments are more likely to lead to occupational disability. In addition, the average earnings of blacks are lower than those of whites. Thus, because of the redistributional component in the benefit formula, blacks are likely to experience less of an income loss by leaving the work force and going on disability.

Cross-Sectional Econometric Studies. Econometric analysis of the population of potential applicants offers a means of identifying the factors most likely to encourage insured workers to apply for DI benefits. The study by Berkowitz, Johnson, and Murphy described in Chapter 4 includes a model for estimating the probability that a disabled male worker will apply.[8] Their study is limited to males in the 1966 social security Survey of Disabled Adults who had insured status in 1965. The Berkowitz-Johnson-Murphy model is based on the presumption that applicants make a choice between regular participation in the labor force and withdrawal, at least to the point at which earnings drop below the limit for DI eligibility. The limit in 1965 was $140 per month. Because the decision to apply for DI is treated in the choice context, variables used in standard labor supply models should apply. A worker going on disability is presumed to

---

[7] Ibid., p. 19

[8] Monroe Berkowitz, William G. Johnson, and Edward H. Murphy, *Public Policy Toward Disability* (New York: Praeger Publishers, 1976), ch. 8.

TABLE 12

APPLICATIONS PER 100,000 WORKERS INSURED FOR DISABILITY, BY RACE AND SEX, 1971

	Men			Women		
Age	White	Black	Other	White	Black	Other
Under 30	264	531	307	114	186	109
30–39	480	1,149	439	462	603	255
40–44	758	1,800	824	708	1,196	494
45–49	1,108	2,545	1,433	1,047	1,826	778
50–54	1,641	3,496	1,794	1,602	2,802	1,430
55–59	2,583	4,426	3,000	2,490	4,568	2,615
60–64	4,753	7,691	4,536	3,651	6,609	3,524

SOURCE: Mordechai E. Lando, "Demographic Characteristics of Disability Applicants: Relationship to Allowances," *Social Security Bulletin*, vol. 39, no. 5 (May 1976), p. 20.

incur an opportunity cost, the loss in earnings that he could have earned if he continued to work. Berkowitz-Johnson-Murphy use the ratio of monthly wages that a worker earned when last employed to the monthly benefit a worker would receive under DI as a measure of opportunity cost. A fall in this ratio toward unity indicates a decline in the opportunity cost of not working. Among the other economic variables included in the model are the wife's monthly earnings in her last job, transfer payments excluding social security, and net value of assets.

In addition to economic determinants of labor supply, the model includes demographic variables that are commonly used in labor supply analyses. Age and education serve as measures of labor force adaptability and skill level. Race is included because of evidence of differences in labor market behavior between races.

Health status is measured by listings of physical limitations in reaching, mobility, and lifting of heavy weights and by condition codes reflecting mental, sensory, and nervous disorders and speech impairments.

In most cases, the results are consistent with the authors' expectations. The coefficient of the opportunity cost variable is negative and significant, indicating that, as the income loss associated with a switch from work to DI increases, the probability that an individual will apply for benefits decreases. In other words, the results support the hypothesis that DI benefits have a work-disincentive effect.[9]

---

[9] Ibid., p. 129.

Effects of the other economic variables are less clear. Wife's income is inversely related to applications. This result was unexpected because a higher earnings potential for the wife would be expected to encourage a disabled husband to take on household responsibilities and release more of the wife's time for labor market activity. Higher asset holdings are associated with lower application rates. While this result may be unexpected, since greater wealth would make it easier to absorb any income loss from going on disability, it is consistent with findings in other studies of labor supply. The usual explanation is that people who accumulate wealth generally possess a stronger motivation to work. Applications are positively related to transfer income, as expected, because transfers cushion the loss from labor force withdrawal.

Applications for disability insurance are related positively to age and negatively to education, although the latter variable is not significant. Blacks are more likely to apply than whites, a result consistent with data reported by Lando, but surprisingly the race variable is not statistically significant. The authors speculate that the race variable may be misspecified, since the model fails to account for interaction between race and other independent variables.[10]

Not surprisingly, the authors find that the presence of physical limitations and functional disorders increases the probability of application. In particular, physical limitations are most relevant in those cases in which the impaired function was a requirement of the worker's last job.[11]

The Berkowitz-Johnson-Murphy study is a useful source of information on why insured disabled workers apply for benefits. The data in their sample are for 1965, however, and the DI program has experienced some major changes since then. These include extension of benefits to workers under age thirty-one and the 1967 revision in the statutory definition of disability. In addition, the application rate among insured workers is now much higher. For these reasons, a study using more recent data is desirable.

In a study completed in 1979, Susan C. Stephenson and I attempt to update the earlier work by Berkowitz, Johnson, and Murphy.[12] This study is based on a subsample from the 1972 Survey of Disabled and Nondisabled Adults. Included are 2,400 adult males aged twenty-five to sixty-four who perceived themselves as impaired and who

---

[10] Ibid., p. 126.

[11] Ibid., p. 125.

[12] Susan C. Stephenson and Charles W. Meyer, "The Demand for Disability Insurance," Staff Paper Series (Ames: Iowa State University, Department of Economics, 1979).

were insured under DI in 1971. A regression equation is estimated to show how a variety of labor supply and health variables are related to the probability that an impaired worker will apply for benefits.

Of particular interest is the test of the hypothesis that a higher level of benefits relative to potential earnings will increase the application rate for DI. As in the Berkowitz-Johnson-Murphy model, the ratio of average monthly earnings to expected benefits is included as an independent variable. This ratio, which serves as a measure of the opportunity cost of forgone earnings, is expected to be related inversely to the probability of applying. The results are consistent with the expectation; the coefficient of the opportunity cost variable is negative and significant at the 1 percent level, as shown in Table 13.[13] Thus, both studies support the hypothesis that male workers with impairments will respond to economic incentives and apply for DI when benefits rise relative to earnings.

With respect to other economic variables, their results show a positive relationship between the application rate and income from transfers (excluding DI) and assets. Both coefficients are statistically significant at the 1 percent level. The signs are as expected, because income from these sources makes it easier for an individual to absorb the earnings loss that accompanies withdrawal from the labor force. The inverse and statistically significant relationship between the application rate and the net value of assets might appear to be unexpected, because persons with greater wealth holdings are better able to forgo earnings. Other labor supply studies, including that of Berkowitz, Johnson, and Murphy, yield similar results, however, indicating that persons with larger wealth accumulations are probably more strongly motivated to work and therefore less likely to apply for DI. Spouse's income and intrafamily transfers are negatively related to the application rate, an unexpected result, but neither coefficient is significantly different from zero.

The results confirm the expectation that older workers and workers with lower levels of education are more likely to apply. The incidence of impairments increases with age, and workers with limited education are less able to adjust to physical limitations or to qualify for sedentary occupations.

Applications are inversely related to number of dependent children, as expected, because such workers are less able to forgo earn-

---

[13] The regression coefficients appearing in Table 13 can be interpreted as the estimated effect of each independent variable on the probability that an impaired worker will apply for benefits. The coefficient of the opportunity cost variable, -0.0518, indicates that a drop of one unit in the ratio of earnings to wages is associated with a 5 percent increase in the probability that a worker will apply.

TABLE 13

PROBABILITY OF APPLYING FOR DISABILITY INSURANCE BENEFITS, INSURED
MALES AGED TWENTY-FIVE TO SIXTY-FOUR

Independent Variables	Coefficient	t ratio
Constant	0.0167	0.26
Economic variables		
Opportunity cost	−0.0518	5.2[a]
Transfer income	0.00003	7.6[a]
Income from assets	0.000018	3.2[a]
Net value of assets	−0.0000004	2.7[a]
Spouse's income	0.00001	0.6
Intrafamily transfers	−0.00002	0.8
Other labor supply variables		
Age	0.0027	3.3[a]
Education	−0.0104	4.1[a]
Number of dependent children	−0.0065	1.1
Rural residence	−0.0036	0.2
Race (white = 0, black = 1)	0.0833	3.0[a]
Health variables		
Limitation in reaching		
Difficulty reaching	0.0928	4.1[a]
Can't reach	0.0925	2.3[b]
Limitation on mobility		
Difficulty walking	0.1269	5.8[a]
Can't walk	−0.1678	2.5[b]
Difficulty using stairs	0.0957	4.4[a]
Can't use stairs	0.1835	4.1[a]
Difficulty stooping	0.0402	2.0[b]
Can't stoop	0.1705	5.2[a]
Can't lift heavy weight	0.0385	2.0[b]
Speech impairment	0.0583	1.4
Mental disorder	0.0791	2.8[a]
Nervous disorder	0.0454	1.2
Sensory disorder		
Hearing	−0.0434	1.6
Trouble seeing	−0.0031	0.2
Trouble seeing with glasses	0.1214	4.6[a]

NOTE: $\bar{R}^2 = 0.278$.

[a] Significant at 1 percent level.

[b] Significant at 5 percent level.

SOURCE: Based on subsample of 2,400 insured males aged twenty-five to sixty-four
included in the 1972 Survey of Disabled and Nondisabled Adults, Social Security
Administration. Data are for calendar year 1971.

ings. Workers from rural areas are less likely to apply, perhaps because of a difference in attitude or in awareness of the program. Neither of the coefficients cited is significant.

Race is entered as a dummy variable, set equal to one for black, zero for white. This variable has a positive and statistically significant coefficient, indicating that blacks are more likely to apply. The result is consistent with the data and explanations provided by Lando and summarized above.

Of the fifteen health variables, twelve had the correct sign and eleven are significant. Generally, the results in the study by Stephenson and myself are consistent with the results reported by Berkowitz, Johnson, and Murphy. Both studies indicate a tendency for application rates to be positively related to the presence of health problems. A notable difference is the strong and significiant positive relationship between nervous disorders found in the earlier study and the positive but insignificant relationship in the later one.[14]

Overall, the economic, demographic, and health variables included in the regression accounted for 27.8 percent of the observed variance in application rates in the study by Stephenson and myself, as compared with 23.4 percent in the study by Berkowitz, Johnson, and Murphy.[15] These are respectable results for cross-sectional samples limited to insured males who reported impairments that limited their ability to work. Primarily because of the differences in data sources, the more recent study does not replicate the earlier one, but both lend credence to the contention that the application rate for DI is in part determined by economic incentives.

Who Is Awarded Benefits?

In an effort to gain additional insights into the award process, Stephenson and I applied regression analysis to the 618 male workers in the 1972 Survey of Disabled and Nondisabled Adults who applied for benefits during 1969, 1970, and 1971. Several health and demographic variables were tested to see which are most likely to increase the probability of acceptance. The award procedure, described in detail in Chapter 3, involves three steps. Insured workers with impairments included in the medical listings, or with impairments deemed to be of equivalent severity, qualify for benefits, unless their earnings exceed the prescribed maximum. During the years in question, the maximum was $140 per month. About 75 percent of the

---

[14] Berkowitz, Johnson, and Murphy, *Public Policy Toward Disability*, p. 129.
[15] Ibid.

allowances are to workers who qualify on the basis of the medical listings alone. Workers who fail to qualify under the medical listings may qualify if they are older workers with limited education and a long history of work in unskilled occupations. Finally, workers may be awarded benefits if, because of physical or mental impairments, they are found to be unable to qualify for a job that exists in the region where they live or in several other regions. Obviously, these criteria become progressively more subjective.

The results are shown in Table 14. The dependent variable is the probability that an applicant is awarded benefits. The coefficients of the independent variables show how each variable is related to the probability of acceptance. Included are nine health and six demographic variables. Because earnings in excess of $140 per month automatically disqualify an applicant, values of the independent variables for any such applicant are constrained to zero. The health variables are: limits to the ability to reach, stoop, walk, climb stairs or inclines, or lift weights; impaired vision or hearing; and speech and mental or nervous disorders. All but two of the health variables have positive coefficients, indicating that they are associated with increased probability of acceptance. Three of them—limitations on reaching, difficulty climbing stairs or inclines, and nervous or mental disorders— are statistically significant at the 5 percent level or better. Two variables, impaired vision and difficulty seeing with glasses, have negative coefficients, indicating that within the applicant population they are associated with reduced probability of acceptance. Neither is significant. Because all of the individuals in the sample are presumed to have serious impairments, it is not surprising that some of the health variables are inversely related to the probability of acceptance. The results may indicate that applicants with limits on the ability to see are more likely than others to have residual capacity to work and are therefore denied benefits. In an effort to measure severity of impairment, a dummy variable was added that was set equal to one if the respondent was totally unable to perform one or more of the functions listed in the survey questionnaire and equal to zero otherwise. Included were total inability to reach, use stairs, stoop, or walk and impairments of vision not correctable with glasses. The coefficient of this variable was positive, as expected, but it was not significant. This result could indicate that awards are not necessarily related to severity of limitations on movement or sight, or that the degree of such limitations is not adequately reflected in survey responses.

Because of the provision in regulations that allows awards to older workers with limited skills, and because impairments often tend

TABLE 14

Probability of Being Awarded Disability Insurance Benefits,
Insured Male Applicants Aged Twenty-Five to Sixty-Four

Independent Variables	Coefficient	t ratio
Constant	0.5112	13.8[a]
Health variables		
Limitation in reaching	0.1214	2.5[b]
Limitation on mobility		
Using stairs and inclines	0.2019	3.1[a]
Stooping and lifting	0.0088	0.1
Difficulty seeing	−0.0155	0.3
Difficulty seeing with glasses	−0.0148	1.5
Hearing disorder	0.0615	0.9
Speech disorder	0.0225	0.2
Mental or nervous disorder	0.1105	2.0[b]
Severity of disability	0.0449	1.1
Demographic variables		
Age at disability	−0.0093	1.5
Age^2	0.0002	2.2[b]
Rural environment	−0.0709	1.4
Education (0–19)	−0.0109	1.6
Number of dependent children	−0.0164	1.0
Race (white = 1, black = 0)	0.0530	0.8

Note: $\bar{R}^2 = 0.14$.
[a] Significant at 1 percent level.
[b] Significant at 5 percent level.
Source: Based on 618 insured males in 1972 Survey of Disabled and Nondisabled Adults, Social Security Administration, who applied for DI benefits in 1969, 1970, and 1971.

to worsen with age, a positive relation between probability of acceptance and age was anticipated. Age at onset of disability and the square of age at the time of the survey are included as age variables. Age at onset is inversely related to acceptance, but it is not significant. The age-squared variable has the anticipated positive sign and is significant at the 5 percent level. The expected inverse relationship between awards and years of education is also observed, but the coefficient is not significant.

A dummy variable for race was included (one for white, zero for black) to test for racial differences in the award rate. As indicated previously, the application rate is higher for blacks than for whites.

One hypothesis is that, because of a lower opportunity cost of leaving the workforce and going on disability, blacks are more likely to apply than whites. If this is the case, and if the same standards of evaluation apply to both races, the acceptance rate would be expected to be higher for whites. The sign of the coefficient of the race variable is positive but not significant, indicating that after adjusting for other factors the difference in award rates between races is not great. Among other demographic variables, the probability of acceptance is positively related to the number of dependent children and negatively related to rural residence. Neither coefficient is significant.

Overall, the acceptance equation explains only 14 percent of the variance in application rates. This result may indicate that information gathered by the survey technique is too imprecise to be useful in a model of the acceptance process, in which the emphasis is on conformity to the medical listings. A similar model tested by Berkowitz, Johnson, and Murphy, using data from the 1966 survey, explained 34 percent of the variation.[16]

Time-Series Econometric Studies

The above evidence indicating that potential applicants for DI do respond to economic factors is based on cross-sectional data collected during a single time period. Data from time series may also be examined to determine the factors affecting the rate of applications and awards for DI. The number of disabled workers receiving benefits has more than tripled since 1965 and more than doubled since 1970. The weighted incidence rate, defined as the number of benefit awards per 1,000 insured males (weighted by age distribution), rose from 3.5 in 1965 to 5.2 in 1970 and to 7.4 in 1975 and 1977. Preliminary evidence indicates that the incidence rate dropped somewhat in 1978, but it remains well above levels of a decade ago. The trends in awards and number of beneficiaries are shown in Table 15.

Several factors may explain the increase in awards. One possibility is a higher level of physical and mental impairment among the working-age population, but this seems unlikely and certainly cannot account for a doubling in the rate of awards. A second possible factor is a relaxation of standards of disability by state and federal agencies administering the program. Other possibilities include a declining reluctance on the part of the public to cease working and apply for benefits or an increase in public awareness of the program.

The importance of economic factors, however, may well be of

---

[16] Ibid.

TABLE 15

GROWTH OF DISABILITY INSURANCE PROGRAM, 1960–1977

	Calendar Year				
	1960	1965	1970	1975	1977
Number of beneficiaries (thousands)					
Disabled workers	455	988	1,493	2,489	2,834
Spouses	77	193	283	453	494
Children	155	558	889	1,411	1,525
Total	687	1,739	2,665	4,352	4,854
Benefit outlays (millions of dollars)	568	1,573	3,067	8,414	11,463
Average replacement rate (percent)[a]	38	37	41	51	52
Weighted incidence rate, males[b]	n.a.	3.5	5.2	7.4	7.4
Estimated long-run cost (percent of covered payroll)	0.56	0.67	1.05	2.41[c]	2.26[d]

[a] Initial benefits as a percentage of previous earnings (highest five years, wage indexed, during ten years before onset).
[b] Benefit awards per 1,000 insured males, weighted by 1977 age distribution of insured males.
[c] Based on intermediate actuarial assumptions.
[d] 1978 estimate.
SOURCE: U.S. Department of Health, Education, and Welfare, "Memorandum for Members of Advisory Council on Social Security" (Mimeographed, September 8, 1978), Item C–1, p. 3.

greatest significance. Replacement rates—that is, the ratio of benefits to previous earnings—have increased on the average more than 25 percent since 1969. In addition, since 1972, workers have been eligible for medicare after two years on DI. Medicare benefits are worth an estimated $1,000 a year, increasing replacement rates by another 25 percent. Consequently, the opportunity cost of leaving the labor force and going on disability is reduced, and an increase in the application rate is to be expected.

The rate of unemployment also affects the application rate. Workers with significant impairments are more likely to become marginal members of the labor force and are, therefore, likely to encounter difficulty finding and holding jobs during recessions. During periods of high unemployment, the DI program becomes an attractive form of income maintenance for impaired workers without jobs.

An increase in applications need not, however, result in an increase in awards. State agencies and the appeals channel in the Social

Security Administration and the federal courts could keep the rate of awards constant by raising the rejection rate. They have not done so, although the rejection rate has risen somewhat over time.

John C. Hambor has constructed a model that uses time-series data to test some of the hypotheses cited above. It is an eight-equation recursive system that determines the number of applications, the initial determinations and denials, the initial allowance rate, total allowances (the sum of initial allowances plus reversals), and the number of awards granted each quarter. The model was estimated using quarterly data for 1964 through 1971.[17]

Hambor's equations for estimating the number of quarterly applications and the rate of allowances are particularly interesting. The applications equation includes as independent variables the unemployment rate for workers aged twenty-five and older, a trend factor designed to capture the effect of slowly changing characteristics of the labor force (notably, changes in age, race, and sex composition), and dummy variables that account for legislative changes and seasonal variation. Two labor supply variables—the ratio of average monthly benefits to an index of private nonfarm wages (a measure of the opportunity cost of not working) and the female labor force participation rate—were dropped because they were insignificant and resulted in a lower coefficient of determination ($\bar{R}^2$). Hambor's results indicate a strong and statistically significant relationship between applications and unemployment. An increase of 1 percent in the rate of unemployment results in an estimated increase of 22,500 applications per quarter from an insured population of 75 million. The applications equation also confirms the expectation that there is a positive trend in the applications rate.

The allowance rate equation shows the expected negative (and significant) relationship between the rate of initial allowances and the rate of unemployment. This confirms the expectation that persons with less serious impairments are more likely to apply when the labor market is sluggish. This equation also indicates that the allowance rate dropped after the 1967 amendment, which tightened the definition of disability, went into effect in 1968.[18]

Hambor points out that, although his model does well in terms of goodness-of-fit criteria, it appears to have some shortcomings. The

---

[17] John C. Hambor, "Unemployment and Disability: An Econometric Analysis with Time Series Data," *Staff Paper No. 20* (Social Security Administration, Office of Research and Statistics, January 1975).

[18] The effect of the 1967 amendment is measured by a dummy variable. The amendment also lowered the age limit for eligibility from thirty to twenty-one, so the dummy may pick up the effects of more than just the change in definition.

failure of the model to show a significant relationship between applications and the opportunity cost variable is disappointing. The reason for this failure, which is not consistent with the cross-sectional results presented earlier, may be the difficulty of adequately specifying opportunity cost in an aggregate time-series model. The model also demonstrated shortcomings when it was used in simulations.[19] Nevertheless, it does provide convincing evidence that impaired workers may treat DI as a form of unemployment insurance. The Hambor model has not been fitted to more recent data, but it lends support to the suspicion that the high application rates observed in recent years, as well as the apparent drop in 1978, may be explained in part by labor market conditions.

A time-series analysis by Mordechai E. Lando yields similar results.[20] Lando used quarterly data from 1962–1973 to estimate two versions of a linear regression model. In one version, the number of applications per quarter is the dependent variable. Independent variables include the number of insured workers, a trend variable, the unemployment rate for married men, and program dummies designed to pick up the effects of the 1967 amendments and the acceptance of Supplemental Security Income (SSI) applications beginning in July 1973. A second version uses the application rate per 100,000 insured as the dependent variable and the unemployment rate, a trend variable, and program dummies as independent variables. All variables except the dummy representing the 1967 amendments are of the expected sign and are significant. The positive sign of the unemployment variable is consistent with Hambor's finding, as is the positive trend variable. Lando speculates that the upward trend in applications is part of the maturing process of the program—more people are becoming aware of its existence and resistance to accepting transfers is weakening. Lando admits that the opportunity cost of DI benefits may also affect the application rate, but he chooses to omit such a variable from his model, citing Hambor's unsuccessful efforts as a reason.[21]

Additional confirmation of the hypothesis that a soft labor market increases the number of DI beneficiaries comes from simulations with an econometric model of the OASDI system. The model, which was devised by members of the staff of the Department of Health, Education, and Welfare (HEW), is a multi-equation system estimated from

---

[19] Hambor, "Unemployment and Disability," pp. 11–18.
[20] Mordechai E. Lando, "The Effect of Unemployment on Application for Disability," *Proceedings of the American Statistical Association*, Business and Economics Section (1974), pp. 438–42.
[21] Ibid., p. 439.

quarterly data for the period from 1965 to 1973.[22] The model is designed to simulate payroll tax revenues and benefit payments to OASI and DI recipients under various assumed economic conditions. In one such simulation, the actual number of disabled workers and dependents drawing benefits at the end of 1977 is compared with the estimated number who would have drawn benefits if the economy had performed in accordance with the optimistic June 1972 forecast of Data Resources, Inc. Data Resources forecast unemployment rates of 5.1 percent in 1973 and about 4.7 percent in the following years. During this period, actual unemployment rates ranged from an annual average of 4.9 percent to 8.9 percent. The HEW model estimates that the higher actual rates added about 700,000 workers and dependents to the rolls, or about 14 percent more than would have drawn benefits if the 1972 forecast had been correct.[23]

Termination of DI Benefits

Although the number of insured workers drawing DI benefits has increased rapidly in recent years, the number leaving the rolls has shown a gradual decline. A comparision of the percentage of beneficiaries leaving the benefit rolls in 1967 and 1976 offers an interesting insight into the effectiveness of rehabilitation efforts. The percentage reaching age sixty-five and switching to old age insurance remained constant at 6.7 percent. The percentage terminated because of death dropped from 8.0 percent to 5.3 percent, perhaps as a result of the gradual influx of younger workers following the lowering of the age limit for eligibility. Terminations because of medical recovery or a return to work declined from 3.3 percent of beneficiaries in 1967 to 1.6 percent in 1976.

Because the beneficiary population includes many older workers with limited skills and education and with chronic ailments that worsen with age, it is not surprising that the rate of recovery and rehabilitation is low. Nevertheless, the decline since 1967 is of concern because it implies higher costs and indicates a lack of success in the state-operated programs of vocational rehabilitation.

The same economic conditions that encourage impaired workers to seek benefits initially may also discourage them from leaving the program and returning to work. Present law allows recipients the

---

[22] A description of the model and selected simulations appear in Lawrence H. Thompson and Paul N. Van de Water, "The Short-Run Behavior of the Social Security Trust Funds," *Public Finance Quarterly*, vol. 5, no. 3 (July 1977), pp. 351–72.

[23] Ibid., pp. 366–67. The authors warn, however, that they have much less confidence in their DI model than in their OASI model.

51

option of working nine months, not necessarily in succession, without loss of benefits. Any month in which earnings exceed $70 is counted as a trial month. Once nine trial months are completed, the worker is allowed benefits for an additional three months, at which time payments cease. A worker who leaves the program in order to return to work also loses medicare benefits (which begin after two consecutive years on DI). To return to the program, a worker must again apply for benefits through regular channels. If he is again awarded benefits within five years of termination, the five-month waiting period is waived, but he must wait another two years for medicare coverage to resume.

These provisions are criticized because they offer inadequate incentive to beneficiaries who might be able to return to work. When the value of medicare is added to cash payments, the average recipient receives benefits worth from $400 to $500 a month. It would take a fairly high earnings potential to induce a disabled worker to take a chance on returning to work, particularly if he runs a significant risk of future layoff.

The limited success of rehabilitation programs may also reflect weakness in the job market. Since seriously impaired workers are more likely to be marginal members of the labor force, they are particularly vulnerable to unemployment brought about by recessions, minimum-wage laws, or economic decline in particular regions or industries. In an effort to encourage state rehabilitation agencies to increase the employability and productivity of DI recipients, Congress in 1965 authorized the Social Security Administration to reimburse states for the cost of rehabilitation services to beneficiaries. Reimbursements are paid out of the DI trust fund. The 1965 legislation limited reimbursements to no more than 1 percent of trust fund outlays. The limit was raised to 1.25 percent in 1970 and to 1.5 percent in 1974.

It was hoped that the reimbursements would be more than offset by savings in benefit payments to rehabilitated workers. Recent studies by the General Accounting Office and Rutgers University estimate that the program saves about $1.15 in benefits for each dollar spent. [24] This figure is much less than earlier estimates by the Department of Health, Education, and Welfare. [25]

---

[24] See U.S. Congress, House of Representatives, Subcommittee on Social Security of the Committee on Ways and Means, *H.R. 8076 Disability Insurance Amendments of 1977,* 95th Congress, 1st session, July 1977, p. 11.

[25] See Ralph Treitel, "Effect of Financing Disabled Beneficiary Rehabilitation," *Social Security Bulletin,* vol. 38, no. 11 (November 1975), pp. 27–28.

The law directs state agencies to require beneficiaries with rehabilitation potential to accept vocational assistance. Those who refuse (except for the blind) can be denied benefits, but such denials are rare. In addition, about 20 percent of beneficiaries are tabbed for medical reexamination in six to eighteen months. If it is determined that a recipient's medical condition has improved enough to warrant termination, benefits cease after three months, whether or not the individual returns to work.

Data on workers who leave the benefit rolls indicate that younger workers, males, and workers with several dependents are most likely to make the transition. Workers who had high earnings before going on disability are more likely to leave the rolls than workers with low earnings, possibly because they have better job opportunities and a weaker work disincentive effect.[26]

---

[26] Ibid., pp. 20–21.

6
Proposals for Revising the Disability Insurance System

The DI program has been subject to periodic revision since its inception in 1956. Most of the major changes have been the result of legislation, and in most cases the changes have involved expanded coverage. Several proposals currently under consideration are designed to reduce program costs and improve the administration of the awards process. The desire to control costs has resulted from the acceleration in the rate of awards and benefit payments that has occurred over the past decade.

In most cases, the suggested changes are linked to a desire to reduce work disincentives, a source of concern in the design of any transfer program directed at working-age persons. Disincentives can be reduced directly by cutting benefits or indirectly by making it more attractive for beneficiaries to return to work. Most indirect means of reducing disincentives require liberalization of eligibility requirements, such as lengthening the trial work period or allowing DI beneficiaries to earn more without loss of eligibility. These changes will reduce program costs only if they encourage enough beneficiaries to return to work for extended periods.

Alterations in program administration are aimed at reducing inequities or delays in the awards process or at improving the generally ineffective rehabilitation program. Questions of federalization of the entire determination process or of stronger federal control over state agencies should be considered before plans for improved administration can be implemented.

Program Changes

The House Ways and Means Committee is considering several major program changes. Specific changes were included in the amendments introduced in the 95th Congress by Representative James A. Burke (Democrat, Massachusetts), who chaired the Subcommittee on Social Security.[1] A memorandum prepared by staff members of the Department of Health, Education, and Welfare for the Advisory Council on Social Security analyzes a number of proposals including those contained in the Burke bill.[2] Most of the proposals discussed in this memo are directed at cutting costs and inducing potential claimants and beneficiaries to work, but some proposed changes would liberalize eligibility requirements.

Proposals to Reduce Costs. The most difficult cases facing personnel involved in initial determination and appeals are those of claimants who fail to qualify on the basis of medical listing alone. Persons who have little education and whose work experience is limited to physically demanding labor are most likely to be affected. Their physical ailments are not severe enough to qualify them automatically for benefits, but their skills are not readily transferable to sedentary occupations. In these cases, it is necessary to make a subjective judgment about an individual's residual work skills. Such cases are more likely to be appealed, and, because of their subjective nature, are more likely to result in inequities among claimants. Total disallowance of vocational factors, now in effect for disabled widows and widowers, could be extended to all claimants. This would disqualify more than 20 percent of those now receiving awards. A less extreme alternative would restrict consideration of vocational factors to workers aged fifty-five and over. This would cut total awards by an estimated 5 percent and, according to HEW, permit a long-run reduction in the DI tax of 0.05 percent of payroll.[3]

Other major cost-cutting proposals involve reduction of monthly benefits. One such proposal calls for calculation of benefits as they are calculated for workers retiring at age sixty-two. Currently, DI benefits are calculated as if the worker were age sixty-five. Use of the early-retirement formula would cut benefits to all disabled workers by 20 percent, but dependent's benefits would not be affected. This change would reduce the current inequity between disability recipients and workers who choose early retirement. The administrative workload would be reduced because workers between ages sixty-two

---

[1] See U.S. Congress, House of Representatives, Subcommittee on Social Security of the Committee on Ways and Means, *H.R. 8076 Disability Insurance Amendments of 1977,* 95th Congress, 1st session, July 1977, for the text and explanatory material on the 1977 version of the Burke bill.

[2] U.S. Department of Health, Education, and Welfare, "Memorandum for Members of Advisory Council on Social Security" (Mimeographed, September 8, 1978), Item C-1.

[3] Ibid., p. 15. Currently 1.5 percent of taxable payroll is allocated to DI.

and sixty-five would no longer have an incentive to apply for DI. As with any benefit reduction, it would reduce the work disincentive effect and cut program costs. HEW estimates that in the long run the adoption of this change would allow a tax cut of about 0.5 percent of payroll.[4]

A less extreme measure involves placing a cap on benefits so no one could receive benefits that exceed net earnings while working. The cap would be set at some fraction of prior earnings. To be effective, the cap would have to apply to total benefits, including dependent's allowances. Present legislation limits the combined payments from DI and workmen's compensation from exceeding 80 percent of average earnings before onset of disability, but this limit does not apply if combined benefits are less than unreduced social security benefits. If the cap were set at 80 percent of predisability earnings, cost savings equal to about 0.1 percent of payroll would eventually be realized, and the worst cases of work disincentive would be eliminated.[5]

Currently, the same formulas are used for calculating both disability and retirement benefits. The 1977 amendments reduced the bias in favor of DI that existed under the old law, but critics point out that the provision that allows the dropping of the five years of lowest indexed earnings from the benefit calculation still favors DI recipients with short work histories. Even under "decoupling," it is estimated that replacement rates will average about one-third more for workers under age thirty and one-seventh more for workers aged thirty to thirty-nine than for older workers. This is because the low-earnings years that can be dropped out are a larger percentage of the work histories of younger workers. One way to reduce the bias would be to prorate the number of drop-out years in accordance with a worker's age or work history. Under one such proposal, workers would acquire one drop-out year for each five years in their earnings history beginning at age twenty-seven, up to the current maximum of five. This change would reduce revenue needs by about 0.05 percent of payroll over seventy-five years.[6]

Proposals to Encourage Rehabilitation. A disabled worker who has not recovered from his disabilities may be discouraged from attempting to return to work by the threat of loss of benefits. Under current

---

[4] HEW, "Memorandum for Members of Advisory Council," p. 10.

[5] Ibid., p. 11.

[6] Ibid., p. 13.

law, benefits cease three months after the completion of a nine-month work period. Thus, a recipient who works for a year (the nine months in the trial period need not be consecutive) has his benefits terminated and must reapply and go through the determination process again in order to return to the benefit roll. Several modest proposals that would relax the existing requirements for continued eligibility are currently under consideration. They include deductibility of selected work-related expenses when calculating maximum allowable earnings, an extension of the trial work period, and a relaxation of the eligibility requirements for medicare coverage.

The DI program is directed only at workers who are judged to be totally disabled and, therefore, unable to engage in substantial gainful activity. Earnings in excess of an allowable maximum—at present $280 a month—are taken as evidence that a worker is not totally disabled, and they automatically disqualify him from receiving benefits. This amount is about half of what a worker could earn by working full-time at the minimum wage. In many cases, disabled workers must incur higher costs than other workers in order to hold a job. To make part-time work more attractive, it has been proposed that beneficiaries be allowed to deduct from earnings the cost of services and devices needed to enable them to work when determining whether they meet the limit on maximum earnings. Only expenses in excess of those incurred by an unimpaired worker would be deductible. The proposed change would make it more attractive for disabled workers in need of support services to work part-time without loss of benefits in the hope that work activity might contribute to their rehabilitation. The earnings limit would not be affected.

Extension of the trial work period would allow beneficiaries to work for more than a year without being dropped from the benefit roll. Although little information is available on the effectiveness of the current trial work period, the House Ways and Means Committee is considering proposals to extend it. The Burke bill includes a provision that would extend the trial period to two years. Benefits would be paid only during the first twelve months, as is now the case. During the second twelve months of work, payments would cease but would resume immediately if the recipient stopped working. The recipient would be spared the delay and risk of denial of benefits that now exist.

In 1972, medicare coverage was extended to DI recipients after receipt of benefits for an uninterrupted period of two years. Medicare ceases when benefits are terminated. Because medicare is ordinarily a valuable asset for persons on DI, the prospect of its loss serves to discourage beneficiaries from leaving the benefit roll and returning to work. Options for dealing with this problem range from eliminating medicare coverage for all workers drawing DI benefits to extending coverage to all former recipients who have not recovered from medical impairments but who have returned to work.[7] The Burke bill contained a provision that would continue medicare through the extended trial work period and for two years after termination. In addition, it would allow the twenty-four-month waiting period for medicare to be nonconsecutive and to be carried over from one period of disability to another. The effect of the latter provision would be to allow workers who were previously eligible for medicare to get coverage immediately if they returned to beneficiary status.

The impact of these proposed changes on program costs is difficult to estimate. Those who proposed them hope that the higher initial costs would be more than offset by long-term reduction in benefit payments, but too little is known about the effect of program parameters on work incentives to make a prediction.

Special Benefits for the Blind. The DI program has traditionally provided preferential treatment for the blind. Existing law waives the requirement for recency of labor force attachment, which requires workers over age thirty with disabilities other than blindness to have worked in at least twenty of the forty quarters before onset in order to qualify for benefits. Blind workers aged fifty-five and over may qualify for benefits if they are unable to work in their previous occupation, whereas other workers must be found unable to engage in substantial gainful activity in any occupation. They are also granted more flexibility in benefit computation procedures, a practice that may result in higher benefits. The 1977 amendments raised the allowable earnings that indicate substantial gainful activity to the amount prescribed for the retirement test for workers aged sixty-five and over.[8]

In recent years, the Senate has considered additional preferential treatment for the blind.[9] These include eligibility for benefits after only six quarters of coverage, regardless of age, the dropping of all years of zero earnings when calculating benefits, and the elimination of all earnings limits as a condition for receiving full benefits. Blind workers would continue to draw benefits even if they refused to accept vocational rehabilitation. Finally, benefit calculation in accord-

---

[7] Recipients who experience medical recovery are terminated regardless of earnings, so no work disincentive is involved.

[8] Currently, the maximum allowed under the retirement test is $333 per month.

[9] HEW, "Memorandum for Members of Advisory Council," pp. 17–18.

ance with the preferential procedures described above would continue past age sixty-five.

No one questions the fact that blindness can add greatly to the inconvenience and difficulty of working or of daily activities. Many blind persons have demonstrated that blindness need not be disabling, however, and the extension of additional preferences to the blind raises serious questions of equity. It is not at all obvious that blind persons have a greater claim on society's resources than other persons with severe and disabling ailments.

Relaxation of Eligibility Standards. The DI program is directed at workers judged unable to engage in substantial activity—payment of benefits is supposed to be restricted to workers who are totally disabled. A slight concession is made to older workers with limited skills and education—those characterized by the "worn-out manual laborer" syndrome. This is a relatively restrictive requirement. If the standards for eligibility are to be relaxed, the most likely options appear to be the granting of benefits to those who are occupationally disabled or to those with partial or short-term disabilities.

Other governmental and private disability programs typically grant benefits to persons who are no longer able to work at their usual occupation. Federal civil service, railroad, and veterans' disability programs and the black lung program for coal miners all provide benefits to those who are occupationally disabled. The only benefits to the occupationally disabled under the DI program are to the blind who are age fifty-five or over. Older individuals who are prevented by blindness from performing an activity requiring skills or abilities comparable to those required in an occupation in which they were previously engaged with some regularity over a substantial period of time may qualify for benefits. The 1971 Advisory Council on Social Security recommended that this provision be extended to all workers age fifty-five and over. The estimated cost would be about 0.5 percent of payroll. Because of the high cost, the 1975 Advisory Council recommended that cash benefits to workers qualifying under this definition be limited to 80 percent of PIA and that they not be allowed medicare benefits. These limitations would cut the estimated cost to 0.13 percent of payroll. [10]

The proposal to put DI on an equal footing with other disability programs, especially other federal programs, has some merit. In particular, it is difficult to justify differential treatment between workers

---

[10] Ibid., p. 16.

on social security and those in the railroad and civil service systems. The difference no doubt results from the industry-specific or employer-specific nature of the latter groups. Whether or not occupational disability should qualify a worker for benefits, one way to insure equity among all workers would be to incorporate federal and railroad employees into the social security system.

Extension of benefit payments to workers who are partially disabled would involve a more fundamental change in the system. Without doubt, workers with physical and mental impairments usually earn less than they would if they were well, and payment of benefits from the DI trust fund would cushion the fall in their standard of living. There are two difficulties with this proposal. First, it could raise program costs enormously. A precise estimate of the cost cannot be made. It depends on a variety of program parameters and, if benefits are in any way related to earnings, on disincentive effects. HEW estimates that the cost could range from 1 percent to 3.5 percent of payroll. Given the strong opposition to existing payroll taxes, an increase of that magnitude would be politically unacceptable.[11] Second, the granting of benefits for partial disability would add enormously to the administrative burden. The number of applications would multiply, and each applicant would have to be assigned a place on the disability scale.

Extension of benefits to persons with short-term disabilities would also add significantly to cost and administrative load. Current law limits benefits to persons whose disability is expected to last for twelve months or longer, and it imposes a waiting period of five months after onset before payments begin. Other transfer arrangements, such as sick pay or workmen's compensation, are better suited to the needs of workers with transitory ailments.

Administrative Changes

Ideally, DI benefit claims should go through a determination process that accurately separates those with residual marketable skills from those unable to engage in substantial gainful activity. The distinction should be based on objective criteria. Claims should be processed promptly so that recipients do not have to wait for payments to which they are entitled. Eligibility standards should be clearly stated and available to the public so that applicants can easily determine whether or not it is worthwhile for them to apply.

---

[11] Ibid., p. 19.

Obviously, no determination process can measure up to such standards. The connection between objective medical characteristics and ability to work is often tenuous. Some individuals with a severe impairment continue to work, while others in the same condition find work impossible. In formulating the medical listings, a subjective decision must be made about whether or not it is reasonable to expect persons with a particular impairment to work. The consideration of vocational factors, which serve as the basis for awards in more than 20 percent of all cases, appears to add an element of subjectivity. If properly conceived, however, the introduction of vocational factors can improve the sorting process. A physical impairment that would be only a nuisance for a clerical worker might totally prevent a manual laborer from working. The new regulations that the SSA is introducing are designed to make the relationship between degrees of impairment and the ability to perform different kinds of work more objective.[12]

Critics of the program contend that a restructuring of the determination and appeals process is necessary if claims are to be treated in a uniform manner. The most radical change would involve federalization of the entire administrative apparatus coupled with a reorganization of the appeals channel. More modest changes would involve increased federal monitoring and supervision of state agencies, changes in the way claims are documented, and changes in the handling of appeals.

Federalization. Initial determinations are now made by state vocational rehabilitation agencies in accordance with federal guidelines. Evidence of lack of uniformity among states is cited above in Chapter 3. Interstate differences exist in personnel rules, training requirements, and organizational structure. Proponents of federalization presume that these differences contribute to a lack of uniformity in the way claims are decided. A major drawback of federalization is the need to transfer to the federal payroll about 10,000 state employees while retaining their seniority and pension rights. The transfer along with the accompanying reorganization would have to be effected without unduly delaying the processing of claims.

A less radical alternative would give the SSA the option of terminating agreements with states that fail to conform to federal guidelines. The termination option would enhance the SSA's ability to encourage uniformity while avoiding the transitional problems of total federalization. This alternative, if accompanied by increased

---

[12] The vocational-occupational "grid" is described in more detail in Chapter 3.

monitoring of the state agencies, should give the SSA substantial leverage in promoting uniformity.

Increased Federal Monitoring. Before 1972, all state determinations were reviewed by the Bureau of Disability Insurance in Baltimore. The SSA has legal authority to reverse awards (but not denials), and the 100 percent review gave federal examiners an opportunity to enforce more uniform standards across states. In 1972, the Bureau of Disability Insurance review was cut to a 5 percent sample as part of an economy move. Critics of the determination process generally agree that the sampling procedure is not effective and recommend a return to reviewing all awards. In the interest of greater uniformity across states, federal review and reversal authority could be extended to state denials as well.

Restructuring the Appeals Process. Claimants who are denied benefits may appeal the decision through three stages of administrative appeal and ultimately through federal courts. In 1977, initial determinations were made in an average of sixty-two days, but cases that passed through each of the stages in the appeals channel took an average of about one year to process.[13] Thus, the appeals process is both time-consuming and costly. In addition, reversal rates are high enough to cause concern. Rather than insure justice, the appeals process may be rewarding persistence.

The administrative law judges seem to be the weakest link. They reverse nearly 50 percent of the denials that reach them and are responsible for an average delay of nearly six months in the processing of appeals. Several factors appear to contribute to the high reversal rate. These judges make a complete reevaluation of the claim and may consider new information not available to state agencies. They offer claimants their first opportunity for face-to-face contact with a decision maker and generally hear testimony of government vocational and medical experts. Claimants may be represented by counsel.

Critics also complain that administrative law judges do not decide cases consistently. Various means are available to promote more consistency among these judges and to reduce their reversal rate. As a starting point, it is hoped that the new "grid" system that relates impairments to capacity to do different kinds of work will for the first time impose a common set of criteria on all persons involved in the

---

[13] HEW, "Memorandum for Members of Advisory Council," p. 2. Only about 2 percent of claims were processed through all three steps of administrative appeal.

determination process. Conformity among judges could be encouraged by systematic sampling and remands by the Appeals Council. Imposition of quotas on reversals would be a more extreme means of promoting uniformity. The gains from the use of quotas must be weighed against the possible loss of confidence in the appeals process should the public gain the impression that judges are no longer independent and impartial.

Some of the difficulties at the hearings stage result from inadequate case development by state agencies. Administrative law judges are forced to seek additional information and to base decisions on evidence that may not have been available to state personnel—a cause of many of the reversals. Among the causes of inadequate case development are heavy case loads, pressures to speed up the determination process, and inadequate supervision of state agencies by the SSA.[14] These problems cannot be eliminated without increased commitment of resources to state agencies and the SSA.

Judicial Review. Applicants who fail to attain benefits from the administrative appeals channel may take the case to a federal district court. Full judicial review adds to the workload of courts and subjects the system to judicial interference in the determination process. Court decisions have on occasion forced Congress to amend the law, and courts can interfere with efforts to promote uniformity in decision making.

One way to deal with these problems is to enact legislation limiting judicial review to constitutional issues and statutory interpretation. Another option, included in the Burke bill introduced in 1977, is to establish a separate disability court to review cases under DI and SSI. In arguing for this provision, Representative Burke cited the rapid increase in the number of disability cases filed.[15] The number now exceeds 10,000 a year, more than the total number filed between 1956 and 1970. A disability court could relieve district courts of this workload and could contribute to greater uniformity in case adjudi-

---

[14] In 1976, the General Accounting Office issued a report that was highly critical of SSA monitoring procedures. The report criticized SSA for failing to identify areas of weakness in the performance of individual state agencies, failing to provide states with the necessary feedback needed to improve performance, and failing to return many inadequately prepared cases to states for review and reconsideration. The report was also highly critical of the way individual states handled quality assurance problems. In response, SSA has taken some steps to correct these shortcomings. For a summary, see U.S. Congress, House of Representatives, Subcommittee on Social Security of the Committee on Ways and Means, *Review of State Agency Decisions*, 95th Congress, 2d session, February 1978.

[15] House of Representatives, Subcommittee on Social Security, *H.R. 8076 Disability Insurance Amendments of 1977*, p. 14.

cations by creating a consistent body of jurisprudence that would be binding on administrative law judges and others in the decision channel.

Other Reforms

The program revisions discussed above would make marginal changes in the DI system and might encourage some disabled workers to seek employment, but they would leave the essential nature of the program intact. A more radical proposal calls for the use of different benefit formulas to calculate retirement and disability benefits. The current formula, with its benefit structure weighted in favor of lower earnings, would apply only to retirement benefits. Disability benefits would be strictly proportional to indexed taxable earnings, and dependent's benefits would be eliminated. The DI program would become a form of pure insurance. Recipients with inadequate income from other sources would receive supplementary income maintenance payments from SSI. Since SSI and DI use the same definition of disability, eligibility should not be a problem. Indeed, about 770,000 DI beneficiaries now receive supplemental transfers under SSI.

The effect of this change on program costs would depend on the level at which the proportion were set. Benefits set at 58 percent of average indexed monthly earnings (AIME) would leave the cost to the DI trust fund unchanged but would redistribute benefits away from recipients with low earnings or with dependents. Setting benefits at 50 percent of AIME would save 0.2 percent of payroll and would reduce disincentives associated with high replacement ratios.[16] If the proportion were set below 58 percent, the payroll tax allocated to the DI trust fund could be reduced, and part of the burden of supporting disabled workers could be switched to other revenue sources. Because of the needs test that is applied to SSI recipients, transfer dollars could be targeted more efficiently to those most in need.

One criticism of this proposal is that, for many disabled workers with a low AIME, it would make the distinction between social insurance and welfare meaningless because once they qualified for benefits they would be forced onto the SSI rolls. Under the current benefit formula, however, more than one-fourth of the workers receiving DI are already drawing additional payments from SSI. Even with the present redistributive formula, the DI program does not provide adequate social insurance benefits for a large number of beneficiaries.

---

[16] HEW, "Memorandum for Advisory Council," pp. 20–21.

If benefits were made proportional to AIME, and if SSI payments were used to supplement the income of beneficiaries with inadequate resources, it is likely that the bulk of the support for disabled workers would continue to come from the payroll tax. In recent years, and particularly since the passage of the 1977 social security amendments, concern has been growing over the increasing reliance on this source of revenue. One reason for concern is the alleged regressivity of the payroll tax. Many economists contend that the full burden of the tax, including the employers' share, falls on wage income. Because of the upper limit on annual taxable earnings ($22,900 in 1979), the tax is regarded as regressive, although the rapid increase in the upper limit makes it somewhat less so. In addition, the earned-income tax credit available to low-income families with dependent children serves to offset the payroll tax for this group. A second source of concern, apparently inconsistent with the assumption that the payroll tax is fully shifted to wage earners, is that it raises labor costs and, hence, contributes to inflation. Consequently, several suggestions for changing the method of financing disability benefits are likely to receive serious consideration.

One option is to supplement all OASDHI trust funds with funding from general revenue. The Carter administration proposed a modest transfer of funds during periods of high unemployment when payroll-tax receipts fall, but this alternative was rejected by Congress. Another option is to finance the entire disability program out of general funds. General funding could be accomplished in two basic ways. One way is to continue to calculate DI benefits in accordance with the existing formula. Benefits would be related to earnings history, but funding would come from general revenues instead of from the property tax. A second alternative is to eliminate the DI program completely and replace it with an expanded SSI program. The latter approach would eliminate disability insurance, replace it with a needs-tested disability program, and in effect return to the 1956 situation.[17]

All of the proposals to restructure the program dramatically force the country to rethink its philosophy of social insurance. If the redistributive component in the formula for calculating DI benefits is eliminated, should the same thing be done for retirement benefits? It would seem to be more consistent to do so, but the two programs differ in at least one respect. DI benefits are paid to working-age adults, some of whom may be able to work, whereas retirement

[17] For discussion of replacement of DI with a means-tested program for the impaired, see Paul N. Van de Water, "Disability Insurance," *American Economic Review*, vol. 69, no. 2 (May 1979), p. 278.

benefits are paid to recipients not expected to work. The major source of work disincentive under DI occurs among low-wage workers with dependents. The combined effect of dependents' allowances and the redistributive benefit formula can lead to replacement ratios high enough virtually to eliminate any monetary benefits from working. This consideration may serve to justify the use of different benefit formulas for retirement and disability.

The proposal to supplement trust funds with general fund financing strikes at the heart of the contributory principle on which social security has been based since its inception. This is an issue of broad social policy and is only tangentially related to the specific issues of disability. The proposal to fund DI out of general revenues without changing the benefit formula is a particular version of the proposal for a supplement from the general fund. It simply sets the share of general funding equal to the share of the DI trust fund in the overall OASDHI program, although it might be interpreted as a first step in the eventual shift of the disability program from social insurance to welfare.

The immediate elimination of DI, and its replacement with an expanded program of SSI, raises serious questions about the willingness of government to deliver on its commitments. Admittedly, persons covered by social security do not have the contractual rights that exist under private insurance contracts, but they do expect that a specified degree of labor force participation will provide them with a degree of income security against medical disability.[18] These expectations in turn are an integral part of the economic environment in which they make plans for their own economic security. Removal of the DI program and its replacement with a means-tested welfare program would be interpreted by many as a violation of a public commitment.

---

[18] Lance Liebman, "The Definition of Disability in Social Security and Supplemental Security Income: Drawing the Bounds of Social Welfare Estates," *Harvard Law Review*, vol. 89, no. 5 (March 1976), p. 855.